HAUNTED NEUK

Other books by Norman Adams

Non-fiction:
Goodbye, Beloved Brethren

Dead and Buried?

In the Dead of the Night

Hangman's Brae

Haunted Valley

Fiction:
Bloody Tam
(with Ninian Reid)

Blood Dirk

HAUNTED NEUK

Ghost Stories of Aberdeen and Beyond

NORMAN ADAMS

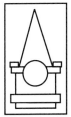

TOLBOOTH
BOOKS
Banchory, Scotland

First published 1994 by
TOLBOOTH BOOKS

The Spinney, Auchattie, Banchory,
Kincardineshire AB31 3PT

ISBN 0 9521738 2 4

**British Library Cataloguing-in-Publication Data. A catalogue
record for this book is available from the British Library.**

Typeset by Bryan Angus, Aberdeen

Printed by BPC - AUP Aberdeen Ltd

CONTENTS

Stage Fright. 'Jake the Ghost' and a Grey Lady haunt His
Majesty's Theatre, Aberdeen, pictured in 1952.

Introduction

'Ghosts Get Everywhere!', was a friend's suggested title for this book. I liked the idea but settled instead for *Haunted Neuk* - neuk being the Scots word to describe a point of land projecting into the sea.

Ghosts get everywhere? During my quest for stories of Northeast hauntings I discovered that old castles and Victorian mansions are not the exclusive domain of phantoms.

I came across reputed hauntings and weird happenings on stretches of road, a wartime airfield, a caravan park, a tramcar, public houses, hotels, a theatre - even a North Sea oil platform!

Did you know Aberdeen once had a 'Street of Ghosts'? It has long been swallowed by the towering St Nicholas House, the City Council's administration block. In old Latin charters the lost street was known as *Vicus Lemurum* - 'Road of the Spirits' or 'Street of the Goblins'. But to later generations of Aberdonians it was better known as the 'Ghostraw, 'Ghaist Raw', 'Gestraw' or 'Guestraw'.

Before the Guestrow became a cluttered car park in the 1960s, it was one of the city's earliest and best known streets. Its name was always a source of mystery. But there seems little doubt that the Guestrow, which was the only street of that name in the country, owed its designation to its location, overlooking St Nicholas Churchyard a short distance away. Before the valley between the graveyard and the 'Ghaist Raw' became honeycombed with houses, residents of the ancient street could glimpse restless spirits flitting about the tombstones at night. Hence its unique name.

There's no mystery why Boathouse Brae in Old Aberdeen got its name. The narrow-tracked right-of-way which ran between High Street and Great Northern Road was associated with the old canal.

But 'Boatie Brae' had an evil reputation... it was dark, lonely and frequented by robbers. Womenfolk would plead with their hosts to allow the tallest boy in the household to act as their escort after dark. A small lad served the purpose just as well for it was said his shadow would satisfy authority!

The brae was also said to be haunted. Its ghost was seen by a lady from Hilton House as she neared the Aulton accompanied by a lantern-bearing groom. They did not tarry long enough to leave us a description of the ghost.

Thankfully, while researching this book - the first to deal entirely with ghosts in Aberdeen and the North-east - I collected a number of first-hand accounts of strange phenomena. Where I investigated traditional hauntings I endeavoured at all times to give them a spectral brush-up.

Norman Adams

FOREWORD

By Peter Underwood FRSA
Life President of The Ghost Club Society

Ghost stories are either fictional or factual. Here Norman Adams presents a formidable array of factual paranormal activity from North-east Scotland, a particular rich vein, it would seem, for research and study.

I am reminded that when I wrote the first gazetteer of Scottish ghosts more than 20 years ago, I was impressed by the quality of firsthand experiences that came my way: the redoubtable Lucy Bruce who claimed to really see 'fairies in her garden'; Sir Shane Leslie whose stories of ghostly encounters in Scotland were legendary; Captain Sir Hugh Rhys Rankin who had seen several ghosts in Scotland; erudite Donald Ross who saw an open-air ghost; Wendy Wood, the Scottish patriot, who herself witnessed the haunting of Ben Macdhui; Sir Peter Masefield who saw a ghost aircraft at Montrose's old aerodrome; and people like speed king Donald Campbell, TV personality Fanny Cradock, Battle-of-Britain saviour Lord Dowding, author Dennis Wheatley and John, Duke of Bedford, who all told me they had personally seen some of the ghosts of Scotland.

Memories flood back as I read some of the chapters of this book. Thunderton House in Elgin, where a former proprietress, Mrs Agnes Brown, heard the unexplained sound of bagpipes and glimpsed a mysterious 'green lady' - why are there so many Green Ladies in Scotland but very few anywhere else? Then there is magnificent Fyvie Castle with its Haunted Chamber, phantom trumpeter and ghostly female form. I knew Mrs Wilhelmena Stirling, whose book on Fyvie Castle is quoted here, when she lived at Old Battersea House where her ghost now walks or did a few years ago when I took a team of investigators there.

Leith Hall, where the somewhat imaginative Elizabeth Byrd had a 'strange and seeing time' had no effect on a later tenant, who was grimly against the 'rubbish' of ghosts! Elizabeth always maintained that when she lived there the house was haunted but today, as you will read, the guides are adamant that the house is no longer haunted - but more than 20 years ago it was a very different story.

We need more sensible books like this, more investigation in this puzzling field, and more careful study of these remarkable and well-attested activities that expose our inadequate knowledge and awareness of the paranormal and it is to be hoped that Norman Adams will extend his excellent studies and research into other areas of haunted Scotland, land of beauty, mystery and enchantment.

Peter Underwood FRSA
Savage Club
1 Whitehall Place
London SW1A 2HD

Chapter One

'Johnnie Ghostie!'

C locks struck midnight, and in a small, red pantiled cottage in a wide courtyard hidden in a maze of streets and wynds of Aberdeen a strange scene was unfolding.

By dim gaslight a group of 12 persons, half of them spiritualists, attempted to bring an end to the poltergeist-like activity that had terrorised a family for almost a week.

The Aberdeen Haunted House Mystery had gripped the imagination of the public at home and abroad, and hundreds of curious onlookers besieged the cottage in the hope of hearing ghostly noises.

The focus of attention was No 1 Gordon Place, a somewhat dilapidated cottage which stood off that part of Old Mill Road that straggles between Bon-Accord Street and Dee Street.

Tenants of the house were laundry vanman Alexander Urquhart, a former artilleryman, his wife and their four children - two boys and two girls. Their son John, a 14-year-old invalid, was singled out by the 'ghost' for special attention when the strange events began on the night of Tuesday, 6 January, 1920. As they prepared for bed at 10 o'clock they were startled by a loud thump on the kitchen wall. This was followed by a deafening crash as though the floor below had been struck by a hammer. The Urquharts knew the basement was empty and barred.

The first 'visitation' lasted nine hours. Crockery rattled in a cupboard; a small dressing table inched around the floor, as well as a child's toy. John's cot bed was raised off the ground by an invisible force before it crashed down. The family were frightened out of their wits and police were summoned. An officer who was first on the scene was in time to catch John, who was half-thrown from his cot by the movement of the floorboards. Knocking and rapping noises seemed to follow the boy around the house, and it was decided the children should sleep at a neighbour's.

The next day the 'haunting' was the speak of Aberdeen and round about. 'Naething wrang wi' the hoose', complained a neighbour, but that was a minority view as spectators, mostly youngsters, flocked to Gordon Place. The Urquharts became overnight personalities, with relatives, reporters and spiritualists invading their tiny accommodation which consisted of a kitchen and two cramped bedrooms.

In the days ahead a number of theories for the ghostly happenings were advanced - trapped sewer gas pushing the house upwards, shifting sand and static electricity from a telephone pole.

Police were convinced the disturbances were caused by structural defects in the house.

It was said the cottages were built for railway workers when the Joint Station terminal opened in the last century. But nearby Gordon Street was laid out in 1800-1807 by Thomas Gordon, a mason, who feued most of it for hand-loom weaving shops. So the 'haunted' house might have been much older and occupied by weavers rather than railwaymen.

The police investigation - it was described by a reporter as a 'perplexing business' - was thorough. On the night of the first disturbances a posse of eight policemen - six constables led by an inspector and a sergeant - minutely examined every floor board and brick of the haunted house. They climbed up a ladder to inspect the chimney and roof.

The disused blacksmith's shop in the basement was given close scrutiny. Wooden uprights supporting the floor of the Urquhart house were described as somewhat shaky by the investigators.

But the public and psychic experts blamed supernatural forces. It was remembered that a former tenant of the blacksmith's shop had committed suicide by poisoning himself many years before. His disappearance went unnoticed until months later his decomposing body was found in a wood near the croft of Hoggin at Countesswells, now a trim suburb on the western edge of Aberdeen.

The strange noises went on night after night. Soon letters began pouring into the Urquhart household from all parts of the country. A firm in Derby even rushed circulars to the city, advertising 'psychic mascots guaranteed to give immunity from the dangers of the spirit world' at 12 shillings (60p) a gross.

Aberdeen City Police Chief Constable William Anderson received offers of help from ghostbusters. The force offered to billet the family at its headquarters at Lodge Walk, but this was refused, although the Urquhart girls eventually lodged with neighbours.

There was a wave of support for spiritualism in the Twenties -

the decade following the blood-letting of the Great War. In Aberdeen, as elsewhere, it was a common practice in the working class areas for women to hold seances.

The creator of Sherlock Holmes, Sir Arthur Conan Doyle, president of the British College of Psychic Science and author of a history of spiritualism, took a keen interest in the Aberdeen haunting.

The Bon-Accord Spiritualist Association held a seance in the house. It took place early one evening and resulted in a number of spirit manifestations. Two journalists were present as the lights of the room were subdued and 13 persons sat down and formed a circle by clasping hands. After hymns were sung a medium made contact with a Gordon Highlander killed in France, and later a fireman. But the lady was not happy with the conditions. The seance was pronounced a failure - due it was claimed to the presence of unbelievers in the large crowd who waited outside the house.

Undaunted, a second seance was planned a few nights later, with 12 persons present. This time at midnight, and this is the story the association later made public.

Their conclusion: The noisy spirit was that of Mr Urquhart's father, a commercial traveller, who had died six years earlier, and who had returned to the world to communicate a message to his invalid grandson, John.

Witnesses had noted that the strange noises seemed to follow John about the rooms, no matter where he went. Experts today say the outbreak of poltergeist disturbances usually occur in a house where there is an adolescent who is disabled.

That John was the target of this psychic energy there was no doubt. And yet?

The seance was held in John's bedroom. The boy shared the bed with his brother throughout the seance. The lady medium sat on the edge of the bed. Present were six sitters - four women and two men, Mr and Mrs Urquhart, the two boys and two witnesses. The gaslighting was lowered. For half-an-hour nothing took place. A sitter whistled a well-known hymn. Shortly afterwards the medium went into a trance, and began passing messages from her spirit guide, an Irishman name 'Paddy'.

'Paddy' told her that the spirit of a man was present in the room, pacing the floor in an agitated state.

Mr Urquhart claimed it was the spirit of his late father. The medium, talking in a thick Irish brogue, explained that when the old man was on his death bed he had called on his son, 'Alec', but he had been 'too weak to communicate the message he had on his lips.'

Astonished witnesses then heard the medium speak in the tongue of an old man. Three times the voice called out 'Alec!'. Mr Urquhart confirmed that these were his father's last words.

After 90 minutes, the medium was drained of energy and the seance ended. The lights were turned full on.

Suddenly, the boy John, who had taken little interest in the seance, sat up in bed, threw his arms in the direction of his father. He said his grandfather was standing at the foot of the bed and laughing. John shouted: 'Oh! daddy, daddy. I ken what it is now; It's granda to tell you to take care o' grandma.'

The boy became hysterical and collapsed sobbing on his bed, his father comforting him.

John later told witnesses: "I was greetin' 'cause I was doon in a black hole, and I was that pleased when I got up and saw the licht and ye a'; I saw granda and he was lauchin'. I got a message but I canna mind what it is noo. I was that feared in the dark.'

Following the eerie midnight seance the atmosphere at No 1 Gordon Place changed. The strange noises ceased as suddenly as they had started.

A city spiritualist announced to waiting pressmen: 'The manifestation proves the theory of Sir Arthur Conan Doyle that the knockings are just the ringing of a psychic telephone bell and that once the message is delivered, the summons of the spirit will cease.'

The Aberdeen spiritualists were pleased with the results of their investigation, a report of which was sent to the Psychic Research Society.

But after the news of the seance was released, a number of spiritualists harboured grave doubts. A well-known Glasgow psychic expert declared that the evidence was unsatisfactory and attributed the boy's vision to the 'excited state of his mind.'

Mr and Mrs Urquhart hadn't any doubts. They became converted spiritualists.

So was the 'Ghost of Gordon Place' a horror or a hoax?

In the late Eighties, an Aberdeen woman, who was born at No

4 Gordon Place, claimed her mother was sent for by Mrs Urquhart when 'things began rattling about the house.'

'According to my mother,' she recalled, 'nothing seemed to happen when they were in the same room as John Boy.'

'My mother went back into his room and caught him in the act of jumping on his bed, and told the woman: "There's your ghost."' Seemingly he had boxes under his bed with springs attached to them. Before this was discovered, police were brought in and everyone who lived in Gordon Place had to prove they lived there before being allowed in.

As a young man, John, it seems, became a figure of ridicule to street urchins. He dressed in a long black coat and bowler hat, and they would call after him: 'There's Johnnie Ghostie!'

In the 1930s the cottages were bought by a family of coach painters, J. Murray Smith, and converted for use as business premises and storerooms.

During the last war the staff kept firewatch in the building and actually slept in the rooms that were supposed to be haunted. Although they were aware of the haunting they never saw or heard anything. From time to time folk interested in the story were drawn to the yard. In the early Sixties a retired policeman who had stood guard outside No 1 at the height of the scare visited the Smiths and told them all about it.

But Johnnie Ghostie's psychic phone will never ring again at No 1 Gordon Place, The old cottage which thrust Aberdeen into the ghostly limelight has long since vanished.

Chapter Two

Terror in Red Well Road

A cold drizzle from the Moray Firth drifted down Red Well Road as lanky teenage schoolboy Christopher Christie hurried through the darkness to keep a rendezvous at Banff Links with his best friend.

It was quarter past seven in the evening of New Year's Day 1990.

A few minutes earlier the 16-year-old Banff Academy pupil had said goodbye to his mother, Mrs Margaret Christie, in their trim bungalow home in Whitehills, the small Banffshire fishing port, west of Banff.

Before leaving Christopher had taken a phone call from his pal, Kerry Pitt, who lives in Banff, the royal and ancient burgh standing at the mouth of the River Deveron. They arranged to meet on Banff Links, a half-way point between their homes, and return on foot to Banff.

After leaving the street lights of Whitehills behind Christopher crossed a main road and then turned left down Red Well Road, a short, narrow, tarmacked road leading to Boyndie Bay.

The road gets its name because of the beehive-shaped building which protects a spring of water. The Red Well is one of several chalybeate springs in Banffshire recognised as having remedial properties and is thought to date back to Roman times. It stands near the end of the road on the brow of the brae leading to the beach. In the 18th century it was a favourite stopping place for Banff people 'taking the waters.'

'I wasn't in the least bit worried, as I had walked the same road in the dark many times before', Christopher told me at his flat in Tillydrone, Aberdeen, where he had just completed a year's course in computing.

But nothing prepared him for what was about to occur - the most terrifying experience of his young life!

He had walked only a few yards along Red Well Road when he was aware of a figure in the darkness ahead. By this time moonlight had struggled through the brooding clouds, and his eyesight is sharp.

Christopher grew uneasy but kept to the left-hand side of the road, while the approaching figure stayed on the opposite side from him.

The boy stopped, cocked his head, but did not hear the sound of approaching footsteps. The figure had melted into the night - or so he thought.

As he walked along the road he experienced a strange phenomena. 'I started getting a sensation of tunnel vision', said Christopher, who told me he had not been drinking and had never experimented with drugs.

'The hairs on the back of my neck stood on end - and I had a tingling feeling.'

Suddenly, the figure of an old woman in black materialized within a few paces of Christopher *and walked straight through his body!*

As the apparition passed through him he was gripped by an 'icy chill'.

'I had two options - either to drop to the ground and curl myself into a ball - or run. I just screamed - and bolted!'

But as Christopher fled homewards his ordeal was only beginning. Incredibly, the phantom reappeared in front of him - and passed through his body a second time!

Terror gripped the teenager as he crossed the main road. Determined to shake himself free of the nightmare, he leapt the fence of a public playfield, thus taking a short-cut to his home in Wilson Crescent. But to no avail. Time and again - Christopher lost count how many times - the phantom confronted him and passed through him. 'After a few strides she would reappear a couple of steps from me and just go into me - I was very, very scared. I did not imagine it - I am not highly imaginative.'

Christopher sped as fast as his legs would carry him across the darkened playing field. The pools of light cast by the street lamps promised sanctuary.

He will never forget that night, and is still able to give a graphic description of the old woman. He said she was under five feet tall. Her whitish face, which had sagging cheeks, was unsmiling. A dark shadow masked her eyes and nose, although she had hair on her upper lip. Her hands were clasped in front of her body.

The woman wore a black lace veil on her head and dark clothes to the ground.

When I spoke to Christopher's mother at her Whitehills home

17

she told me: 'He was petrified with fear. When he arrived home his heart was beating like mad. 'Mum, I've just seen a ghost!', he said. I said: 'You must be joking, son', but he looked like one!'

Mrs Christie, who is a midwife at Banff's Maternity Annexe, added: 'Christopher was in a terrible state of nerves. I took him in my car to meet his friend Kerry, who was still waiting for him at Banff Links.'

The frightening events of that January night have left their mark on Christopher. He will never again set foot in Red Well Road after daylight. When he visits his mum at week-ends he refuses to sleep in the dark. A short time after the ordeal he was asleep in his darkened bedroom when he suddenly found himself fighting for breath. He switched on his bedside lamp and was in time to see a 'dark cloud' drift towards the curtained window, and vanish.

Mrs Christie told me: 'He came through to my bedroom and said, "Mum, there's something in my room - I could not breath." He was so scared. I have absolutely no idea who or what he met on the road. I feel whatever my son met in Red Well Road that night followed him home.

'From his description it seems the old woman was wearing clothes of the 18th or 19th century. I looked up books in the local library to find out if something terrible happened in Red Well Road in the past, but I was unable to find out anything.'

The road, as I discovered, is a lonely spot even on a warm summer day with sunlight turning the Moray Firth bright silver.

The Red Well itself is an interesting structure, spoiled, when I visited it, by a rash of graffiti. The water trickles deep red - giving strength to the old superstition that impending tragedy resulted in some springs turning to blood, The well provides shelter and a seat for the weary traveller. It is not hard to imagine days of yore when folk included the well on their route of other spas in the Banff area.

So whose ghost haunts Red Well Road?

Our ancestors worshipped wells in ancient times believing the waters could bring luck, fertility or cure various ailments, from toothache to eye disease, and worse. After the Reformation the Kirk punished persons who revered springs, but it proved a losing battle, for in the middle of the last century pilgrims still made their way to such spots.

The superstitious country folk believed the holy wells were

protected by a spirit, embodied, perhaps, in a fish, frog, or even a fly.

But wells were guarded by old women. A gift was given to the crone who had charge of the saint's wooden image at St Fumack's Well at Botriphnie, near Keith, but she could not have done her job properly for during a spate it was swept away by the flooded Isla.

So was the old woman who confronted Christopher Christie the wraith of a long-forgotten guardian of the Red Well?

It's an intriguing thought.

Whitehills did have a character well versed in the ways of magic and the supernatural. In the early 19th century Lily Grant, known as the wise woman of Whitehills, was regularly asked for help by rich and poor alike. A nobleman, believed to be James, Earl of Fife, was driving in his carriage, when his horses became restive and then stood stock still, and no whipping or coaxing would make them budge. Witchcraft was blamed. The animals had been 'reistit'. So Lily was summoned and taken into the carriage with the earl and the spell was broken.

On another notable occasion Lily was asked to cure a bewitched cow at New Deer. She prophesied the animal would speak its tormentor's name. The cow died before that startling event could happen and Lily stuck the cow's heart full of pins and then burned it at a dykeside. The farmer turned down Lily's offer to make the witch responsible dance over the beast's grave!

Chapter Three

Phantoms of the Opera

As I watched a version of *Phantom of the Opera* at His Majesty's in Aberdeen, my mind turned to the ghosts which are said to haunt the theatre.

The Grey Lady has been known to flit across the foyer. But her connection with the theatre is unclear.

'Jake the Ghost' is a more homely sort of phantom than the one which figures in Gaston Leroux's piece of Grand Guignol.

Edi Swan was a student at Gray's School of Art in nearby Schoolhill when he became associated with the theatre as a scenic artist. The year was 1955. Edi became a schoolmaster, but when he retired from His Majesty's in 1993 he was technical director.

His Majesty's Theatre was opened in Rosemount Viaduct on 3 December 1903, but it did not claim a ghost until the second world war. A stagehand was tragically killed by a stage hoist during a circus performance in 1942.

'If anything mysterious occurred we'd blame it on 'Jake the Ghost', Edi told me.

As resident scenic artist, Edi was used to working alone at night. There were occasions when he would break off painting and place his brush on a sink. When he went to pick it up the same brush lay several feet away on a work table.

'I put it down to weariness - my mind playing tricks on me, but I began to make a point of concentrating harder on what I was doing with the brush, so I know it wasn't happening purely by accident.'

So if a brush went missing an exasperated Edi would shout: 'Come on, Jake - will you leave my brushes alone!' It worked.

Edi never actually saw 'Jake' - but some stagehands claimed seeing the ghost on the bridge to the fly floor. Phantom footsteps were also heard.

It is said when 'Jake' walks along 'Lambeth Walk', a long dark passage leading from the balcony to the fire escape stairs at the St Mark's Church side of the theatre, the temperature plummets to freezing. Even though the passage has radiators it is always cold in the corridor.

In 1980-82, while His Majesty's was undergoing extensive

refurbishment, a night watchman, nicknamed 'Skipper', had great difficulty in getting his huge Alsatian guard dog, 'Savage', to enter 'Lambeth Walk'. It proved an impossible task. As soon as the animal approached the corridor it sat back on its haunches and lay his ears back, while his hackles bristled.

'When the watchman reported the problem he was having he had not heard about the theatre ghost,' said Edi.

But there is a more serious side to Edi's dealings with 'Jake' - the two occasions when the ghost acted like a guardian angel.

While working on his own late at night during the 1958-59 season Edi stumbled and fell down some stairs. He was in agony and he feared he had broken his left ankle. He needed a doctor urgently. In those days Aberdeen Royal Infirmary's Accident and Emergency unit was centred at Woolmanhill, only a few hundred yards from the theatre's rear exit.

But the door of the scenery dock was always, but always, securely locked with chain and padlock. The resident stage manager, Bert Ewen, was very methodical in everything he did, and there was no way the door would be unlocked.

Edi groaned at the second option facing him. The alternative route was by a tortuous flight of steps to the top of the darkened theatre, and then down to the front entrance. Even if he had reached Rosemount Viaduct two more streets had to be negotiated before he reached the hospital.

Edi decided to risk the first option. 'Yet,' Edi told me, 'when I reached the exit the chain was off and the padlock open. I could not believe my luck. But when I told Bert Ewen the next day he was adamant he had padlocked the door.'

The other bit of good news was that Edi's ankle was not broken - but it was badly sprained.

Edi's 'guardian angel' came to his rescue another night he was working late on stage. Yet again the scenic artist was alone.

Edi was spraying gold paint on scenery when the nozzle jammed. 'I stuck a pin into the hole to unclog the paint when it exploded in my face,' he recalled. 'I was blinded, and I knew I had to get to a sink and wash my eyes.'

Although in great pain and in a dazed condition, Edi began to crawl to the props room where he knew there was a water tap. But the safety curtain was up and there was the danger he could have crawled blindly downstage and plunged into the orchestra pit.

21

But somehow he groped his way to the sink. 'Jake' helped me that night,' said Edi.

His Majesty's, which is owned by the City of Aberdeen District Council, is one of the most beautiful theatres in the country. Before undergoing its refurbishment many of the strange noises - creaks, groans and bumps - were blamed on the old system of man-handling scenery. With new technology the noises stopped.

But no doubt 'Jake the Ghost' still stalks 'Lambeth Walk,' and other parts of His Majesty's, as he keeps a protective eye on staff, performers and public.

Chapter Four

Alone - in a Haunted Castle!

On a stormy night in the autumn of 1963 a young Aberdeen woman journalist packed her Gordon tartan travelling bag and set off for Druminnor Castle to keep a rendezvous with a band of ghosts.

Lynn Montgomery had agreed to spend the night in the haunted castle - alone.

'It all started as a prank - a dare,' she recalled, 'but during the night I was absolutely petrified!'

Some of her woman colleagues at the Aberdeen *Evening Express* had decided to write about facing their greatest challenge. One writer was rescued by firemen. Lynn's original ideas of going on a trawler trip, or spending two days on a desert island off the West Coast, were given the thumbs down. Editor Robert Smith, the well-known Aberdeen author, suggested she stayed a night in a haunted castle.

Lynn contacted the Hon. Margaret Forbes-Sempill, the laird of Druminnor, near Rhynie in Aberdeenshire, one of the oldest castles in North-east Scotland, and she liked the idea.

From 1271 the Forbeses lived in a 'motte and bailey' fortress - a structure of earthwork and timber. In 1440 Alexander, the first Lord Forbes, moved into the new castle built by John of Kenlock and William of Inverkip of Renfrewshire. Traces of the original castle still exist.

After she acquired the castle and estate in 1955, Miss Forbes-Sempill set about restoring the castle. Tons of rubble were shifted; plaster walls stripped and even the dungeon was rescued from the ignominy of being a coal cellar!

The bedroom where the Duke of Montrose slept on the eve of the Battle of Alford had become a bathroom. The task took nine years. Miss Forbes-Sempill was assisted by a lifelong friend, Miss Joan Wright, of Inverkeithny.

On the appointed night, Lynn and photographer David Sutherland, were given a guided tour of the castle by Miss Forbes-Sempill. After taking his pictures David left for Aberdeen.

Lynn remembers: 'I was given an enormous bunch of keys by

the laird. I had the choice of locking myself in with the ghosts or leave the door unlocked so that I could do a hasty moonlight flit if I saw one. Miss Forbes-Sempill even left me the keys of her Jeep.'

Lynn acquired a guard dog during her vigil - a black labrador named after the nearby river Bogie.

The intrepid reporter bedded down in the castle's 'Happy Room' (christened, it is believed, by King James II), which is directly under the haunted banquet hall.

The hall, according to legend, was the scene of a ghastly massacre by the Clan Forbes, hosts to 15 members of the Clan Gordon, their deadly foes.

The outrage was but one more cruel and bloody deed involving the two clans since the 16th century. In 1571, Druminnor Castle was looted and extensively damaged by the Gordons after the Battle of Tillyangus. In the same year Margaret Forbes, the wife of the absent laird, their children and servants, 27 persons in all, perished when bleak and lonely Corgarff Castle in Donside was put to the torch by a Gordon raiding party led by Captain Ker, a tragedy which gave rise to the poignant ballad, *'Edom o' Gordon'*.

In an attempt to end the long feud influential members of the Clan Gordon met the Chief of the Clan Forbes and his kinsmen in Druminnor Castle.

John Grant, author of *Legends of the Braes o' Mar*, takes up the harrowing story:

'After much argument, the difference being at length made up, and a reconciliation effected, both parties sat down to a feast in the hall, provided by the Forbes chief. The eating was ended, and the parties were at their drink - the clansmen being of equal numbers, and so mixed, as had been arranged, that every Forbes had a Gordon seated at his right hand. 'Now,' said Gordon of Huntly to his neighbour chief, 'as this business has been so satisfactorily settled, tell me, if it had not been so what it was your intention to have done?' 'There would have been bloody work - bloody work,' said Lord Forbes - 'and we would have had the best of it, I will tell you: see, we are mixed one and one, Forbeses and Gordons. I had only to give a sign by the stroking down of my beard, thus, and every Forbes was to have drawn the skein from under his left arm and stabbed to the heart his right-hand man'; and, as he spoke, he suited the sign to the word, and stroked down his flowing beard. In a moment a score of skeins were out, flashing in the light of the pine-torches held

behind the guests, In another moment they were buried in as many hearts.

Realising his mistake the aged chief wailed: 'Sic a peety. O sirs, sic a peety!' But a retainer snarled: 'Damn the peety! It'll tak a lot o' Gordon bleed to droon the auld fire o' Corgarff!'

Four hundred years later the chilling episode filled Lynn Montgomery's thoughts as she settled down for the night in the storm-battered castle. 'For no apparent reason I suddenly realised that my overnight grip was made of Gordon tartan. Panic stricken, I wondered if that would encourage a visit from any of the fifteen.'

Shadows cast by candlelight and a log fire danced a wild reel on the barrel-vaulted ceiling of the room.

'I felt far from brave,' said Lynn.

'Suddenly I heard a noise and froze in terror.' Lynn relaxed. The grandfather clock was responsible.

As she pulled the rugs over her head, trees waved wildly in the high, howling wind beyond a large window.

Lynn wrote: 'I was in the middle of cursing my stupidity for failing to get sleeping pills from my doctor when I heard a thud. A second or two later it came again. I shot a look at the dog, but she didn't seem in the least perturbed. As I dived further into the bed I heard it again.'

Lynn managed to drop off, and the next morning she and Miss Forbes-Sempill set about investigating the thudding noise. 'We could find nothing to explain the cause,' Lynn told me.

In 1963, I spoke to Miss Forbes-Sempill about the ghosts, and she claimed Druminnor was the 'most haunted castle in Scotland.'

Sadly, the charming lady was killed in a road accident near the castle in 1966.

But there is another strange, but touching, story associated with the castle.

Before her tragic death, Miss Forbes-Sempill had suggested to Mrs Lilianne Grant Rich, of Aberdeen, that she write a song or poem about her beloved Druminnor.

Mrs Rich visited the castle and had her photograph taken in the grounds. When she showed the picture to a friend with psychic powers the other woman 'saw a cavalier in 17th century costume standing beside Mrs Rich in the picture, although to normal view she was alone.'

Mrs Rich's thoughts turned to Montrose's stay at the castle. The

25

result was *The White Rose of Druminnor*, a song dedicated to the memory of Miss Forbes-Sempill, and performed for the first time at the Royal Scottish Country Dance Society's Festival Concert in Aberdeen Arts Centre in June 1968.

Chapter Five

Road Hazards

E very summer holiday before the Great War the grandparents of Miss Margaret Frater let their home in Stonehaven to a family from Glasgow.

Margaret's grandfather, Edwin Pithie, and his wife and bairns would then head for their summer retreat - a cottage near the slopes of Craigneil, an 870-feet high hill lying to the east of the Slug Road.

The Slug Road, the A957, links Deeside with the Mearns. This ancient Mounth road which takes its name from the Gaelic word 'slochd', meaning pass, was notorious for robbers in bygone times.

It is also haunted by a weird apparition known as the 'Green Witch'.

Margaret Frater's grandparents knew nothing of the 'Green Witch' when they first occupied the old cottage, which was about seven miles from the town.

Mr Pithie, who owned a plumber's business, and his family, stayed in the country for two months. They were well prepared, transporting all their worldly goods and supplies, by pony and cart. Mr Pithie would commute between Stonehaven and the cottage on foot. A penny farthing bicycle of boyhood was replaced in time by a motor cycle with side-car.

Late one evening in July Grandfather Pithie and two companions were walking back to the cottage when they met the 'Green Witch'.

They were on the long stretch of road that runs for one mile between the Blue Lodge of Ury Estate and Rickarton.

Miss Frater, who is a retired nursing sister, told me: 'The three of them were deep in conversation when all of a sudden a lady dressed in green appeared in the middle of them.

'She didn't utter a single word as she walked beside them. They didn't speak to her. She walked with them for quite a way and then she simply vanished.

'My grandfather and his friends were amazed. They could find no explanation for the strange happening. They just couldn't grasp what had occurred. Cynics claimed the illusion was caused by drink - but this was denied.'

Half-a-century later the ghost was spotted by two Banchory men as their heavily-laden lorry rumbled homewards up the steep incline of the Slug Road.

Raymond Munro was the driver and his father-in-law, John MacDonald, was the passenger.

Banchory historian and writer V.J. Buchan Watt, reporting the sighting in 1956, said: 'Suddenly Mr MacDonald saw what appeared to be the figure of a woman in the headlights.

'She was dressed in a dark green cloak or coat - was of slim build and was standing at the left of the roadside.

'What is a woman doing by herself in this isolated spot? was the thought in Mr MacDonald's mind. Was it a trick of the light?'

He made no immediate comment to his son-in-law. 'But,' said Mr MacDonald, 'he swung the lorry over to the right - so he also had apparently seen the strange figure.'

The green-clad figure seemed to 'draw into herself' as the lorry approached.

And then - as they watched, the figure melted into thin air while the lorry was about 15 yards away.

Both men were convinced they had seen 'someone' and when elderly Banchory resident Hugh Innes heard their strange tale, he didn't bat an eyelid. 'Aye, they must have seen the witch!' he commented.

Mr Innes, who knew the Slug Road intimately, claimed the ghost had appeared at a spot on the road known as 'The Witch's Well'. Deep in a rocky gully on the opposite side of the road wayfarers would find the Witch's Cave.

The old man claimed the 'Green Witch' had confronted many travellers in the past.

A Banchory coachman called Dow was traversing the 'Slug' with a hearse when the strange figure materialized at the side of the road. His horse panicked and by the time Dow had quietened the animal the 'Green Witch' had vanished.

The legend of the Green Witch is well-known in the district. I spoke to a Durris woman who was born at Mergie House and she recalled how as a young girl in the late 1940s she cycled to the summit of the Slug Road and drank from 'The Witch's Well', situated on the east side of the highway. She recently sought out the spring but could find no trace of it, not even a trickle.

Who was the 'Green Witch'? A 13th century poem tells how

Fergus of Galloway made off with a fabulous shield guarded by the Green Witch of Dunnottar Castle.

Her ghost haunted Cumberland House and surrounding streets and wynds in Stonehaven's auld toon until 1948, when the ancient building was reduced to rubble.

The 'Green Witch' has wandered far and wide since being made homeless. Apart from being spotted on stretches of the Slug Road there was a reported sighting in recent times near Laurencekirk.

In late autumn 1961 I was driving back from Balmoral Castle with a newspaper colleague when a white horse, mouth gaping and tail flying, suddenly appeared in the headlights of our car opposite Crathie Church. There was no time to swerve as the beast galloped at us. There was no collision and no sign of the beast in the rear mirror. Pressmen in the car behind saw nothing. Inquiries revealed that no one in the area owned a white horse.

A business friend had an equally mysterious encounter while travelling home to Banchory on the South Deeside Road in the autumn of 1988.

It was dark, damp and around midnight when the lights of his car picked out a horse-drawn coach descending a steep brae near Ardoe House Hotel.

The coach and four horses did not slacken pace at a road junction but continued across the main road before vanishing into a beech hedgerow at the side of the road. The businessman thought the coach belonged to an enthusiast until he realised he had not seen a driver or passengers!

Chapter Six

Seeing Things?

Young children figure in the world of the supernatural. In a haunting by a poltergeist, an adolescent child, usually a girl, is the centre of activity by the noisy ghost.

I remember a case in the Rosemount district of Aberdeen when a policeman summoned to a house, where a young person lived, was met at the door by 'flying plates' hurled by an unseen hand.

But children have experienced eerie 'happenings' other than disruptive poltergeist phenomena.

A well-known North-east journalist, the late Ron Main, told me of a strange episode that occurred during his childhood at Lossiemouth. It happened in his uncle's house in the early 1930s.

Ron's uncle had died a short time before and he was spending the night in the house. The boy and his uncle had been great friends.

During the 'wee sma' hours' Ron wakened in the darkened bedroom. A spherical shape - a white 'woolly blob' was how Ron described it - appeared at the top of the closed bedroom door and drifted towards him.

The 'thing' passed silently over his head and went out the window above him and into the garden. 'I was quite frightened, but not terrified,' recalled Ron. He discounted a suggestion that it might have been a form of ball lightning. He was convinced the phenomenon was connected with his late uncle.

Consider the bizarre apparition Neil MacKenzie saw in his bedroom of the family's fourth floor flat in Aberdeen's Great Western Road.

Young Neil awoke in the middle of the night to see something weird in the old-fashioned mirror hanging on the bedroom wall.

'To my surprise,' Neil told me, 'I was staring up at the white shimmering figure of a man sitting on a horse. Half of the horse was in my room while its legs vanished into the floor.

'The man held what looked like a lance or large stick in his hand. The head of the lance was hidden in the ceiling, while the bottom of the lance disappeared through the floorboards.

'I stared at the image for about ten seconds, then hid my face in the bedclothes. When I had regained enough courage to look in the mirror, the figure had gone.'

To this day Neil doesn't know who or what was responsible for the apparition.

Neil continued: 'I have told a few people about it over the years. Most say it was childish imagination. One person suggested it was a trick of the light - somehow an image had been projected onto the mirror by the lighting on the street below.'

Childish imagination? A trick of the light? Or a ghost? Choose carefully!

Ghosts can be as real and solid as any mortal. And they don't necessarily have to appear in the dead of night.

Michael Ross, who lives in Peterhead, was a toddler when his mother took him to Aberdeen beach. It was a bright and sunny day as they walked past the Mercat Cross in the city's ancient Castlegate.

They had reached the top of Justice Street when Michael looked across the street. 'I saw a woman dressed in what I later learnt was Victorian clothes,' Michael told me. 'She was carrying a parasol, wearing small spectacles and she smiled at me.

'I remember saying to my mother, "That lady is smiling at me", and my mother replied there was nobody there. Nothing exciting - but it remains a vivid memory!'

Chapter Seven

High Spirits

All was quiet in the lounge bar of the Cocket Hat public house in Aberdeen.

The last customer had gone and the doors leading to the main bar and lounge were securely locked. Staff went about their duties, stacking freshly cleaned glasses for the next day's business.

Waitress Agnes McInnes, 22, tidied up in the lounge, which was dimly lit and deserted, before going into the toilet. When she returned there was a strange man standing near one of the pillars.

He was wearing a long coat and a hat.

Said Agnes: 'At first I couldn't believe it. The place had been cleared but here was this man standing alone and silent.

'I went behind the bar but I had to go back and look again. He was still there in the same place.'

Agnes hurried into the kitchen and told the pub manager Alex Cormack. 'He came back with me into the lounge but the man had gone. At first he thought I was having him on but then I described what the man was wearing and where he was standing.'

The young woman's description of the stranger fitted almost exactly that of this former boss, John Walker, who built the Cocket Hat in 1955.

Mr Cormack was dumbfounded.

For Mr Walker had been dead for more than 14 years when he suddenly appeared in the lounge that night in May 1973.

Mr Cormack explained to Aberdeen journalist Bill Harris: 'He always wore a long coat and a hat with brim turned up. He had his regular seat at a table on the exact spot where the girl said she saw the man.'

At first, Mr Cormack refused to believe Agnes. But her description was too close for comfort and he was impressed by her sincerity. Agnes would only have been a child when Mr Walker had died so there was no way she could have known his description.

'When all the staff were finished and had gone home I decided to make another check of all the toilets and any other possible hiding places,' added Mr Cormack. 'Usually my dog comes along with me but that night I couldn't get him to move from his box.'

The manager made a thorough check of the building, locking up as he went. He was satisfied there was no one on the premises.

'I worked for Mr Walker and he was a tremendous guy,' he told Harris. 'He had a son who was killed in a car crash in Malaya.

'I think Mr Walker was hoping his son would take the pub over. I remember him saying after his son's death that the Cocket Hat would be nothing more than a monument to him.

'That's why we kept his name over the front door - for sentimental reasons. It's almost as though the old boss had come back to see how things were going.'

Agnes McInnes was furious at herself for not speaking to the unexpected customer.

'I only wish I had had the presence of mind at the time to speak. Just to say something.

'If anything like this happens again I know I'll try and say something. The man in the lounge looked at me and I was looking at him but for some reason I couldn't describe his face properly afterwards.

'And yet for all that I knew he was an old man. I just wish I could explain it. A lot of people don't believe me I know that, but I wish they wouldn't laugh because I know what I saw and it was real.'

Readers of the Aberdeen *Evening Express* must have rubbed their eyes when the story of the strange encounter appeared in the paper few days after the 'visitation'.

It carried a photograph of a man in hat and coat leaning against a pillar in the Cocket Hat's lounge. But this was no attempt to hoodwink the unwary. The editorial driver had agreed to act as a 'stand-in' spook to add to the atmosphere of the story.

The Cocket Hat takes its name from the triangular piece of land on which it was built at North Anderson Drive. Mr Walker, who had previously owned the now defunct Harriet Street Bar, made a little bit of licensed trade history by opening the Cocket Hat, the first new pub in Aberdeen since World War Two.

But has Mr Walker deserted his beloved Cocket Hat? I wonder. I've been told that some members of staff still 'feel a presence' in the lounge bar. There have been occasions when they were aware of seeing 'something out of the corner of the eye.'

The strangest incident occurred more than five years ago when a down-to-earth barmaid saw a whisky glass moved by an unseen hand across the top of a table in the lounge. The table was dry and not sitting at an angle.

What induced this unnerving action? Imagination? Tiredness? Or was it an example of psychokinesis - the unexplained movement of objects from one place to another?

In summer 1994 staff at the Four Mile Inn at Bucksburn, Aberdeen, were said to be baffled by 'strange noises' after closing hours.

It was reported that two barmen were locking up one night when they heard 'pronounced footsteps' coming from an upstairs area they had previously secured. They checked - but could not find the cause of the sound. On returning downstairs the footsteps resumed.

A pub spokesman admitted: 'The cook had heard strange noises and a customer who had been coming in for 50-odd years maintains this has been going on for a long time.

'I don't know if I believe in the supernatural but I can't think of a feasible explanation for these noises.'

One possible solution from a former customer suggested it was the ghost of an owner in the 1950s who loved a good joke at the expense of brewery reps and passing trade customers!

Two of Aberdeen's oldest pubs are reputed to be haunted.

Cameron's Inn - popularly known to generations of pubgoers as 'Ma Cameron's' - is an old coaching inn and, until 20 years ago, its links with the days of the stage-coach and the horse were very much in evidence - the cobbled courtyard and stables with stalls bearing the names of former occupants.

The inn was built near the end of the 18th century and was formerly Sow Croft.

Mention the name, 'Ma's' to older patrons and it conjures up the clatter of many feet on the flagstoned passage, and the heady perfume of an excellent malt and smouldering peat fire in the front 'snug' on a winter evening.

Before the last war Mrs Mitchell succeeded her late husband as a licensee and the little old lady was often erroneously called 'Ma Cameron' (The Cameron family was associated with the hostelry for six decades).

The quaint pub is still a favourite haunt - in more ways than one!

Alison Bruce, joint owner of Cameron's Inn, has not had a close encounter with the supernatural but she told me of two intriguing incidents.

The first occurred some years ago when a decorator was

working alone in the old lounge bar. Because it was inconvenient for him to paint during opening time it was agreed he would do the job during the early hours.

The man was painting the ceiling when he was startled by three sharp knocks on the floor of the room above. The room had been empty for some time. It was also sealed because it was not being used. He knocked back and the knocks were repeated. For a second time he rapped on the ceiling above his head and the response was identical. The man did not turn a hair but carried on with his work.

The other incident concerned a woman cleaner who reported for duty one day and was met with a 'presence' - 'a sudden drop in the temperature', was how she described it.

The Old King's Highway in the Green stands on the site of a 13th century Carmelite Friary, which was despoiled during the Reformation, around 1560.

Archaeologists have found a host of interesting artefacts in the area - lengths of lead piping which had supplied the monks with water, a well-preserved bronze spigot or tap, the earliest known evidence of plumbing in Aberdeen, a coin, a bone gaming dice and the stone foundations of the church.

The grisliest find was made in 1981 when excavations revealed a mass grave of early Aberdonians - 126 skeletons of men, women and children.

The Old King's Highway may be haunted by the ghost of a monk, which was seen next door in a building occupied at the time by Shirlaws Motor Cycles.

Around the time the excavations were being carried out in nearby St Martin's Lane, a young storeman Mark Griffiths was alone in an upper floor stockroom.

'I had climbed three feet off the floor when I turned my head to see a figure of a monk level with me', Mark told me.

Mark, who now works offshore, said the apparition appeared very solid and wore a brown or grey cloak (The Carmelites, an order of begging friars, were known as the White Friars because of their dress but they later donned a dark-brown habit).

'Although it was hooded I could see its face - it was the face of an old man,' added Mark.

The ghost disappeared after 30 seconds. 'I got a bit of a scare,' he said. 'When I told my mates they did not believe me.'

Mark's former boss, Roy Shirlaw, recalled: 'When Mark came downstairs his face was as white as a ghost. He said he had seen a ghost!'

Roy never saw the phantom monk but he told of a curious incident when mechanics failed to remove a stubborn metal nut from a bike. When they reported for work next morning the nut had been inexplicably loosened. Before moving to new premises Roy said he heard noises in the building but added: 'I have an open mind on the subject of ghosts.'

Next door at the Old King's Highway they've heard of the ghost monk. The apparition has not been seen in the pub but an eerie presence is sometimes experienced. Owner's son Sean Stewart told me: 'At times you think someone is watching you - it's ever so strange.'

Does a ghostly Carmelite monk haunt the pub and neigbourhood?

Perhaps it is the restless wraith of Brother John Tulford, who was in charge of the White Friars in the burgh when it was ransacked during the Reformation? He and his brethren survived the outrage but Brother Francis of the nearby Trinitarian establishment was not so lucky. The Red Friar was butchered by the mob and his body tossed into the burning monastery.

Moray boasts a famous haunted pub.

The ancient royal burgh of Elgin has a history of witches and ghosts. In more barbarous times persons suspected of witchcraft were drowned in the 'Order Pot', a deep, dark pool near Elgin Cathedral.

Ghosts were given a wide berth.

An Elgin mansion, Calder House, built by Provost Thomas Calder in the 17th century, had a dark reputation when owned by a physician, Dr Alexander Dougal. Tales of a wailing ghost and the 'boiling of dead bodies in cauldrons' were circulated by superstitious townsfolk.

Years after Dr Dougal's death the house, with turrets to the High Street, remained a tenantless ruin where the hideous wraith of 'Nelly Homeless' stalked the long winding dark stairway. The haunted house was removed in 1820 to make way for North Street.

Centuries-old Thunderton House, the former town residence of the Earls of Moray, was occupied by Bonnie Prince Charlie a few weeks before his defeat at Culloden in 1746.

His hostess was Lady Arradoul, eldest daughter of Dunbar of Thunderton. According to her dying wish, she was shrouded and buried in the bedsheets which the Prince had slept in during his stay.

Thunderton House underwent many changes. From smart town mansion it became a church, furniture warehouse, preaching station, windmill and in modern times - a hotel.

Past owners of Thunderton House Hotel claimed it was haunted. The sound of bagpipes and voices were heard and on one memorable evening witnesses saw a standard lamp lift a foot in the air and move across the room of its own volition. When it reached the other side it landed with a thump but remained undamaged.

Thunderton House, in a lane off busy High Street, is now a public house, its former bedrooms no longer open to the public.

Hauntings are rare nowadays but the people at the Thunderton put me in touch with Ewan Mennie, who worked there before moving to the licensed trade in Aberdeen. Ewan told me of two odd incidents which took place in the Elgin hostelry.

A barman was in the cellar at night when a heavy plastic curtain parted. There was no one there. Was it a trick of the wind? The frightened man did not linger.

A member of staff was counting takings when a bundle of banknotes, held in place by a rubber band, flew into the air.

No headless phantom. No gibbering Green Lady, but disturbing enough if you were alone in a haunted pub.

Ewan has his own theory about the resident spook. He believes it is the ghost of Lady Arradoul, and not Bonnie Prince Charlie, that haunts Thunderton House.

High spirits are not only to be found in Aberdeen's hostelries.

The Old Custom House at Aberdeen Harbour is supposed to be haunted. A disembodied voice, a ghostly figure and an eerie presence have all been reported in the past.

There is no mistaking the elegant Georgian mansion in Regent Quay. Over the front door is the sun-burst motif of the Sun Fire Insurance Company, a reminder of the days of private fire brigades. The house was built by an unpardoned Jacobite, James Gordon of Cobairdy, in 1771. He died two years later and the mansion was eventually sold by his son to the Collector of Customs.

In the late 1950s a young man on night duty became aware of an 'icy presence' in the room.

And another officer was alone in a ground-floor office one night when he heard a strange voice utter: 'Ah, there you are.'

Twenty years ago an officer was also on his own in the building at night when he glanced up from his easy chair to see 'an ethereal figure with a woman's face' bending over him.

Chapter Eight

The Ghost in Room One

In the summer of 1994 an elderly man armed with divining rods arrived on the doorstep of the Pannanich Wells Hotel, near Ballater, and told the owners: 'I believe you want to get rid of your ghosts!'

'No we don't,' protested Val Norton, 'they're lovely!'

Even so the Nortons allowed the visitor to have a look round. Did he find any ghosts? He didn't see any spooks - but felt their presence at various 'cold spots' throughout the hotel.

Val and her husband Chris experienced strange happenings in the old coaching inn when they took over in 1987.

Room Number One at the back of the hotel had an 'uneasy' feeling when they first arrived, Val told me. She promptly lodged a menagerie of teddy bears belonging to her and her daughter Alisha in the room. 'The atmosphere changed instantly', said Val. 'It is really a happy room.' Disembodied breathing has been heard in the room and the smell of violet scent detected.

But not all guests would agree. Some have been known to book out in a hurry. A United States travel agent said several of her clients returned from Pannanich claiming there was a 'strange aroma' in the room.

Chris met one of the hotel ghosts five years ago. He dubbed her 'The Grey Lady'. 'I looked up one day and this strange lady was standing at the top of the stairs,' he told me.

He said she was young-looking, slim, and dressed in a long, dark skirt and grey blouse. Chris has a theory that she is the spectre of a Victorian maid. 'She is a friendly ghost,' he added.

Does the Grey Lady haunt Room One? A young American couple cut short their stay in the haunted room after they complained of 'a large grey stain' on the bedspread - but there was nothing wrong with it!

A far cry from sensational claims in the tabloid press that men were queuing up to book the room - to spend the night with a 'sexy ghost in a saucy maid's outfit'!

Mysterious noises have been heard in other parts of the hotel, and a former owner told the Nortons to expect to confront another phantom - a young boy begging for water!

Perhaps the boy is hoping for a drink of the spa water that has made Pannanich Wells renowned for the past 200 years? Famous historical figures who have 'taken the waters' were a young Lord Byron and Queen Victoria, who wrote fondly of 'the curious little old inn', in 1870, where her faithful servant John Brown had previously worked for a year.

Chapter Nine

Into Thin Air

During the early evening of 25 October 1940 the Luftwaffe - Heinkel bombers of KG26 in Stavanger - attacked the RAF station at Montrose, Angus, bringing death and destruction - and incinerating a highly-confidential dossier on a famous haunting.

The complete file detailing the case history of the Ghost of Montrose Aerodrome was locked in a safe in the Adjutant's Office in the Officers' Mess.

When the safe, radiating heat, was forced open that night, the documents had turned to ash, along with wads of banknotes which were to have been paid out to personnel!

But the oldest ghost story in aviation did not go up in smoke. Although sometimes the subject of pure speculation and sheer invention down through the years, it is one of the most baffling hauntings on record.

Birdsong had long replaced the roar of aircraft engines when I visited the site of the old aerodrome at Broomfield on the edge of Montrose Links to talk to local man Ian McIntosh, secretary and treasurer of Montrose Aerodrome Museum Society.

The Society was formed in 1983 mainly to protect Major Burke's sheds - hangars built before the outbreak of World War One and reputed to be the oldest structures intended to house military aircraft in the world.

It was Mr McIntosh who told me about the fate of the 'Ghost File'. His informant was his father, William, an ex-Royal Flying Corps pilot, who, during the last war was a telephone engineer in Montrose. 'The file on the hauntings was deliberately suppressed for reasons of morale,' said Ian.

Because of the many telephone lines in use by the military, including the RAF, and the pressure of the war, Ian's father, now deceased, spent days on the airfield and at St Cyrus radar station.

Ian McIntosh recalled how as a boy in Montrose an evening's outing to one of the town's two cinemas would sometimes end abruptly with his father being summoned by the RAF.

'I remember dad being called out by the film being stopped, and his name and the message being flashed on the screen. The film

41

then started, but dad had to go, leaving me and mum, or sometimes just me, alone for the rest of the film.

'Mum always wondered if dad would be alright knowing he was working on the site of a potential bombing raid, but luckily we all survived, despite being bombed out, and machine gunned. Others in Montrose were not so lucky!'

The legend of the Montrose Ghost was familiar to airmen in both world wars, and in peace-time. New staff on arrival at the station, which was closed in 1957, were officially told in writing that the place was haunted.

The 'ghost' inspired flying folklore. It was said it was some kind of guardian angel between the wars, safeguarding the life of a crashed pilot. But in wartime an airman who felt its soft tap on his shoulder could be sure he would not survive the next flight.

The story began on 27 May 1913 when a BE bi-plane piloted by Lieutenant Desmond Arthur of the Royal Flying Corps suddenly folded up in the air above Lunan Bay, south of Montrose, and crashed into a field.

Spectators watched in horror as Lieutenant Arthur was thrown from the aircraft and plunged 2500 feet to the ground. He didn't stand a chance, for it would be another 14 years before the RAF introduced parachutes. An investigation eventually revealed the Irishman had been the victim of a criminally negligent repair to a wing of his tiny aircraft. Arthur was a member of No 2 Squadron RFC, the Premier Heavier-than-Air Squadron, which four months earlier had begun operations at a new airstrip at Upper Dysart, Montrose - Britain's first operational military air base.

In those early days officers and men of No 2 Squadron were billeted at the old Panmure Militia Barracks near Montrose Harbour, on the south side of the town.

It was here that the ghost of a pilot in flying kit was seen in or around the Officers' Mess. There were reports of the apparition vanishing as it reached the doors of the mess. It was also seen in the mess, sometimes sitting in an armchair. Soon the story spread that it was the ghost of Desmond Arthur.

In 1934, the April issue of *Popular Flying* carried an astonishing letter on the haunting by Major P.L. Holmes, DSC, late of the RNAS and RAF.

The court of enquiry into Arthur's crash found that it was due to pilot error, wrote Holmes. But the dead man's relatives were not satisfied by the findings and a second inquiry cleared Arthur's name.

Major Holmes wrote: '*The strange feature connected with this was that from soon after the publication of the finding of the first court until the second court published its finding a strange officer kept appearing to other officers in and about the officers' quarters at Montrose and vanishing completely as suddenly as he had appeared.*

'*Pre-war and early wartime pilots of the RFC, who had not yet been subject to the mental strain of flying over the lines, were not exactly the sort of people whom one would expect to see things that were not there, yet numbers of these officers saw the ghost, and in some cases it appeared in the night in rooms shared by two officers and was seen by both.*

'*One has not met anybody who openly disbelieved in the Montrose ghost at the time of its appearances, and even the War Office tried to hush the matter up.*

'*It was generally believed in the flying services at the time that the ghost was, in fact, Desmond Arthur endeavouring to get the finding of the court of inquiry on his accident altered, and it was largely due to the ghost that the original finding was altered by a second court.*'

When operations were switched to the present aerodrome at Broomfield the hauntings did not fade. Uncanny incidents took place in the vicinity of Waldron Road Bridge at the main entrance on the west side of the drome.

In 1936 an RAF policeman, Norrie Webster, was on duty one dark night when he heard the sound of footsteps ahead of him. His flashlight failed to pick out the intruder. Undeterred, the policeman gave chase. The footsteps sounded ahead of him. Their trail led past the corner of the old hangars, where he was in time to see a curtain of hosepipes, draped on a wall, shake.

He headed back in the direction of Waldron Road Bridge where the intrepid policeman was given a nasty shock. The footsteps rapidly approached him from out of the darkness. He stood his ground and shone his torch. The footsteps stopped a few feet from him *but there was no one there!*

Webster wasted no time in reporting the weird incident to his sergeant in the guardhouse.

I heard of two other classic manifestations of the ghost, both occurring in 1942.

43

Ian McIntosh told me that during the last war a NAAFI building stood on the western edge of the drome. It was an informal place and air and ground crew would nip across for a quick cuppa. It was common for pilots to call wearing their flying suits before going back to their billets.

On this particular day airman Alex Kettles and his colleagues heard a 'dreadful scream' coming from inside the wooden building. They rushed indoors to find the NAAFI girl unconscious on the floor behind her counter.

It seemed that on hearing the friendly roar of an aircraft landing, she got ready to open for business. She poured tea then threw open the shutters. A pilot in a flying suit strode towards her. Just as she held out a welcoming cup he vanished. She fainted.

In the winter of the same year Alexander Hendry, a civilian night fitter, spoke to the ghost!

Mr Hendry - described by his son Tom as a 'phlegmatic sort of Scotsman' - worked for the Air Ministry Works Directorate. On the night in question flying had been scrubbed because of fog and low cloud. Mr Hendry was on his way from the workshop at the south end of the drome to the airmens' kitchen. To get there he had to cross Waldron Road Bridge, spanning the Bervie branch railway line, and close to the spot where policeman Norrie Webster heard phantom footsteps six years earlier.

Tom, who now lives in Aberdeen, told me: 'As my father started to cross the bridge he could make out a figure in flying clothing walking towards him. As the figure passed, my father made some comment about the weather, but got no reply. When he looked over his shoulder, the figure had completely disappeared!'

His father quickly checked the surrounding area but there was no trace of the mystery flier - and not a sound to break the stillness.

That night it would appear Tom's father, who is now deceased, had joined the ranks of those who had come face to face with the ghost of Lieutenant Desmond Arthur. Or did he?

Some ghosthunters have claimed there are two or more ghosts at Montrose - the wraith of Lt. Arthur and the spectre of a World War Two pilot killed in a crash.

Ian McIntosh favours the two-ghost theory but with a slight twist. He believes Arthur's ghost was confined to the Militia Barracks. The apparition that haunts the old drome, he believes, is not Arthur's ghost, although it belongs to the same flying age.

To establish the identity of the ghost of Broomfield one need only begin in 1983 when the Montrose Aerodrome Museum Society launched its Hangar Fund to save Major Burke's sheds.

Three girls who visited the old drome by car claimed they saw an apparition hovering in the vicinity of the pre-World War Two hangar. By a strange coincidence a hangar from the time of the Great War stood at this spot.

An Australian psychic and clairvoyant, Tom Wards, who was visiting his mother in nearby Brechin in August 1990, accepted an invitation to investigate the sightings at the old hangar.

His conclusion seemed bizarre - at first. The ghost, he claimed, was the restless spirit of a prankster who liked dressing up in flying uniform. He sensed the person had suffered from insanity.

There is a connection between the RFC and the old Montrose Lunatic Asylum.

Ian McIntosh recalled that the old asylum had stood in present-day Garrison Road, and was latterly used as the Panmure Militia Barracks, home to No 2 Squadron before the outbreak of World War One. Indeed a plaque marking the site is fixed to the wall of a former hotel, which was the commanding officer's house.

Desmond Arthur never flew from Broomfield - the RFC moved there from Upper Dysart in late 1913, six months after his death.

So whose ghost is stalking the drome at Broomfield?

Ian believes it might be that of Major F.F. Waldron, who was killed in France in 1916. The name of the pioneer flier, the first pilot to land at Upper Dysart, lives on in the bridge and adjoining road.

Ian and his younger brother Graham, vice chairman of the Museum Society, have visited the graves of Waldron and fellow officer Major C.J. Burke, his former CO, who lends his name to the sheds. Photographs of their graves can be seen in the Society's museum, a timber building that has survived two world wars and several bombing raids.

Indoors there is a fascinating collection of memorabilia - flying gear, model aircraft, maps and old photos, including those of the wreck of Desmond Arthur's plane, and his funeral cortege.

Outdoors there is a range of old aircraft, including a Vampire jet, and helicopters. Incredibly, the members salvaged bits of propellers from a Fairey Barracuda which had seen service as a garden fence!

The museum, which was the station headquarters in the last war and subsequently used by the Department of Transport driving examiners, also has a reputation for being haunted.

In November 1987 Alistair Hill told the *Dundee Courier and Advertiser* of mystery footsteps he and his fellow examiners heard in the building.

'I believe most of my colleagues over the last ten years will have heard these footsteps,' said Mr Hill. 'There is no doubt - they are footsteps we hear.'

The footsteps, reported the newspaper, were heard every year, usually in late afternoons in November/December.

'We are usually sitting in the office when we hear the footsteps of someone coming in at the front door and walking along the wooden floor. When we get up to see who has come in there is nobody there, or outside.

'It's been going on for at least ten years and we just accepted it, although we have to keep checking just in case it is someone coming in.'

In 1994 Ian and Graham McIntosh were decorating the building when something odd took place. Ian was painting the ceiling of the display room while Graham was outside. Ian heard the sound of a door opening and footsteps approaching along the corridor. The sound ended in another office. Ian checked, but he was alone. Graham was up a ladder creosoting the roof, unaware of the mystery caller. 'I wasn't in the least bit frightened,' Ian told me. 'I just accepted it.' Then there was the time Graham was alone in the building when someone rattled the handle of the front door. Graham threw open the door but there was no one around. He was puzzled. For there had been something strange about the noise - it sounded like the rattle of an old-fashioned door knob - and the present door is fitted with a modern handle. There was another occasion when the Museum Society's chairman David Butler and his son Neil were in the museum and Neil swore he saw a shadowy figure flit into an office. But the ghosts of Montrose are not confined to dead fliers. In the early Eighties a woman was driving her car on Rossie Brae, outside the town, when a plane swooped overhead. Because of her husband's interest in aviation she recognised a Hurricane fighter of the last war.

Although it was so low she could make out the rivets on its fuselage and wings the plane made no sound. She braked but the mystery plane had disappeared. A check of RAF records revealed that two Montrose-based Hurricanes had crashed into the bay during the war.

Yes, there would appear to be something strange in the air at Old Montrose Aerodrome!

Chapter Ten

Ladies in Green

Muchalls Castle, north of Stonehaven, is shrouded by mature trees on a hilltop within cannon shot of the North Sea.

This delightful L-shaped house was built in 1619 by Alexander Burnett of Leys, the same man who completed Crathes Castle.

In early summer 1990 Muchalls sprouted a second castle when Italian filmmaker Franco Zeffirelli arrived to direct Mel Gibson in *Hamlet*. Scenes were shot around the clifftop movie-set, and at Dunnottar Castle, while Ophelia spent a few uncomfortable hours in the Muchalls Burn!

But there is only one Muchalls Castle, described by respected author and historian Nigel Tranter as 'part of Scotland's unique heritage in stone and a comfortable home into the bargain.' The castle boasts magnificent and delicate plaster ceilings in the reception rooms and a stunning Great Hall, featuring an ornamental fireplace with a sculptured overmantel dated 1642 and bearing the Royal Arms of Scotland.

The original laird's bedroom has a secret 'laird's lug' and a gold and crimson canopy reputed to have been slept under by James VIII and III, 'The Old Pretender'.

There is a wishing well in the cobbled courtyard which is protected by a curtain wall set with gun-loops on each side of the turreted gateway.

Muchalls, a country house hotel, where guests can experience a real sense of Scotland's history, is also reputed to be haunted by at least two ghosts - a Green Lady and a Yellow Lady. But it has been suggested that there might only be one ghost, whose dress is beginning to fade with the passage of time.

This might not be so fanciful as it sounds.

In December 1962 the last thing Alistair Reid expected to see after an enjoyable evening at the farmers' ball in Stonehaven Town Hall was the castle ghost.

Alistair was the guest of Maurice and Geraldine Simpson, who were then the castle owners, and it was arranged he would spend the night in the Victorian wing.

It was three in the morning when Alistair bade goodnight to his hosts and climbed the stairs to his bedroom. To reach his room Alistair had to cross the dining room, now a drawing room.

The dining room was in darkness when he pushed open the door, but daylight filtered in through the windows. There was a table in the centre of the room and as he entered the figure of a woman was moving across the floor on the far side of the table. She was walking from left to right in the direction of a cupboard, which years later would reveal a secret passage.

The strange lady vanished in the blink of an eye.

'I felt the hairs on the back of my neck stand up,' Alistair told me. 'It was a terribly frightening feeling - one I have never experienced before or since.

'The figure was not wearing green - the clothing was light,' said Alistair, who, being an interior decorator in Aberdeen, has a craftsman's eye for such things.

His hosts laughed off Alistair's story at breakfast next day but he told me: 'I actually think it was a ghost I saw. I have never been in any doubt about it.'

Mrs Glenda Nicol Cormack, who was educated in Elgin and Inverness, fell in love with Muchalls after 18 months of fruitless searching for a Scottish house to suit her and her business partner.

I spoke to her about the reputed hauntings in the cosy drawing room, the very room in which Alistair Reid glimpsed the ghostly apparition all those years ago.

'I do believe in ghosts,' Mrs Cormack said frankly, 'but I don't feel anything here.'

But she did tell me one strange story which apparently happened in the early 1950s. A woman caretaker was alone in the castle when she heard a tremendous noise. She thought the owners had returned unexpectedly but on checking found there was nobody about.

Lord Robertson was Lord Justice General of Scotland when he lived in the castle towards the end of the last century.

And thereby hangs a tale of the Yellow Lady, told to me by Mrs Geraldine Simpson.

During the time the Simpsons owned the castle they had a visitor whose father had been a guest of Lord Robertson around 1906. The visitor told Maurice Simpson, sadly now deceased, that his father had been delayed for dinner because his train was late in arriving at Muchalls Station.

Dinner was about to be served but when the late arrival hurried to the dining room he saw a girl in a 'yellow frock titivating in front of a mirror' when he passed a bedroom below his. On reaching the dining room he commented on not being the last down to dinner and was told that he was, and that there was no such guest fitting the description of the mystery girl.

Mrs Simpson, who never saw or heard anything supernatural during her years at the castle, told me: 'We were unable to discover the room in which the guest saw the lady in the yellow frock.'

The steep, cave-pitted cliffs at Muchalls were a haven for smugglers in years gone by.

The fishermen of the lost village of Seatown of Muchalls had a reputation for smuggling gin into the country, until a great storm around 1794 destroyed the fleet and brought total ruin to the community. Legend has it that a huge tidal cave at Muchalls was connected to the castle, more than a mile away, by an underground passage. A piper once marched into the cavern - and has not been seen since, although on a stormy night you might hear the sound of his ghostly pipes!

The Phantom Lady is said to be the restless spirit of a girl from the castle who drowned while going down the secret passage to meet her smuggler sweetheart at the mouth of the cave.

The castle entrance to the tunnel is believed to be beneath the stone-flagged floor of the present dining room. Mrs Cormack has carried out some preliminary excavations, without result. So far!

Several other North-east castles and great houses have a Green Lady stalking their property - Crathes Castle, Drumtochty Castle and Culter House, to name a few.

Sixteenth-century Crathes Castle has a room named after its famous ghost, the figure of a young woman wearing a green robe and nursing a baby.

A young girl gave birth to a child fathered by a servant but vanished mysteriously with her charge. The father slipped away from the castle and was never seen again. In the last century a small skeleton was found under the hearthstone of the Green Lady's Room, where strange things still happen.

Elsewhere in the Mearns, the Green Lady of Drumtochty is reputed to haunt the main front staircase of the 19th century castle during the month of May.

A Green Lady is said to haunt a bridge and burn at Durris. She is the wraith of Lady Durris, who drowned herself after her husband was murdered and their home and crops burned by the rampaging forces of the Duke of Montrose in 1645.

A phantom of similar appearance caused generations of Scouts sleepless nights under canvas at Templars' Park, Maryculter. According to legend a Saracen maid and her lover, Godfrey Wedderburn, were slain by his Knights Templar brethren. Result: A bolt of lightning killed the Templar chief - and if you find the legend hard to swallow 'The Thunder Hole' can still be seen at Maryculter today.

A Green Lady was included in the sale of a Banchory property just after the Second World War!

In April 1949, 18th century Castle Airy House, a three-floored Category B-listed building fronting the town's High Street, was Lot 76 in the sale by auction of Banchory Estate.

The schedule stated: 'The house is well-known to Banchory residents as originally it was built for the local doctor and much mystery has been attached to the legend of the 'Green Lady', who is reputed to still haunt the house.'

I spoke to a Banchory lady whose mother tenanted the house at the time of the sale. She informed me: 'We knew of the legend but I never saw the Green Lady when I lived there and I don't think my mother did either.'

At the turn of the century local bairns would avoid the steep path bordering the house, built in 1750, rather than face the wrath of the Green Lady.

Modern youngsters are less afraid, it seems. When the present owners, James and Winifred Rourke, moved in 10 years ago children would knock on their front door and ask to see the resident spook!

Mrs Rourke told me none of the family had spotted the ghost, so perhaps the Green Lady, like the legend, is fading...?

It would appear to be a different story at the scene of the most famous Green Lady haunting in North-east Scotland........

Chapter Eleven

'The 'Green Ladye o' Fyvie'

The 'Green Ladye' has flitted through the corridors and halls of Fyvie Castle for almost four centuries.

She is said to be the ghost of the wife of Sir Alexander Seton, a notable Laird of Fyvie, and Godson of Mary, Queen of Scots. But woe betide anyone belonging to the family of the reigning laird who saw her. Her sudden appearance was said to portend death or calamity.

Seton married Lilias Drummond in 1592, They had five daughters, but no son or heir for the laird. Lilias died and within six months the laird had wed the young and beautiful Grizel Leslie. It was said their wedding night, in the chamber now known as the Drummond Room, was ruined by heavy sighing from outside the room. The next morning the name of the laird's dead wife was carved upside down in three-inch high letters on the outside sill, high above the ground.

In 1879, as his brother Cosmo Gordon lay ill, Captain Alick Gordon was confronted by the family ghost, emitting a faint iridescent glow, in a gloomy passage. The phantom curtsied, and Alick fled in terror. He burst into a room where his wife was sewing and said: 'I have just seen the Green Lady, and she hailed me as the new head of the house! Cosmo will die!' The new laird outlived Cosmo by only five years.

Poor Alick dreaded the apparition and once flew into a rage when a guest appeared at a castle party dressed as the green phantom. As events turned out, his reaction is understandable.

On his deathbed in the Gordon Room, traditional 'dool chamber' of the Gordon lairds of Fyvie, Alick told his wife that he had again seen the 'Green Ladye.'

In 1918, an army captain, a 'hard-headed, shrewd materialist, who had no belief in anything supernatural', was invited to convalesce at the castle. During his stay at Fyvie the officer, who was a Canadian mining engineer in peacetime, slept in the Gordon Room. Not a happy choice as it turned out. On his arrival he was full of banter, but as the days progressed he became silent and ill at ease.

It transpired that he had been awakened every night by a mysterious light in his bedroom. The light grew brighter and he could make out details of the pictures on the walls. The first time it happened he thought he had forgotten to switch out the lights. He got out of bed and found to his amazement that he had turned them on!

After several sleepless nights the officer quit the castle before breakfast! It was established he had been ignorant of the legend of the 'Green Ladye.' The phenomena of the Gordon Room was also experienced by the brother of Lord Leith, another laird, who said of ghosts: 'Never combat the Supernatural, meet it without fear, and it will not trouble you.'

The 'Green Ladye o' Fyvie' sounds a fearful phantom, every bit as terrifying as the other castle 'horrors' - the cold hand that wakened sleeping guests; ghostly footsteps on the great staircase, stifled shrieks in the dark; a secret chamber, the Curse of the Weeping Stones and indelible bloodstains on the floor of the Douglas Room, the former 'Murder Room'. Oh yes, and not forgetting a ghostly trumpeter, Andrew Lammie, who wooed the doomed Agnes Smith, 'Tiftie's Annie', the miller's daughter.

In January 1920 members of the castle staff disclosed further hauntings.

A maid, Miss Massie, was wide awake in her bed at five one morning when a 'white object stepped out from the wall near the head of my bed. I could not make out the features, but the figure was that of a lady dressed in a wide, flowing white gown. I was too terrified to speak. She sailed straight across the room, and looking round at me, as I imagined, before she left, disappeared into the door opposite.'

So it seems the 'Green Ladye' has a rival!

Miss Kellas, the housekeeper, reported frequently hearing 'thuds, knocks, and moaning , for which no reasonable explanation was forthcoming.'

'We thought,' said Miss Kellas, 'that the sounds came from the ballroom, which is almost right above our bedrooms, but the most careful search showed nothing that could possibly account for them.' A former maid corroborated her story, while another girl told me how a hatbox inched slowly along a shelf until it was on the point of toppling over the edge, before she snatched it.

In her book, *Fyvie Castle, Its Lairds and their Times* (1928), Mrs

53

A.M.W. Stirling, opined that spectres and legends had fallen on hard times with the advent of modern life.

Perhaps she was whistling in the dark, even if she maintained the castle's haunted stairways had been illuminated by new fangled electricity.

Did Fyvie's 'Green Ladye' fade from the scene - exorcised by the electric light bulb? Then again, perhaps she only changed her modus operandi?

It is an interesting theory, backed up in an interview I had with an Aberdeen woman who was brought up in Fyvie before the last war.

Mrs Betty Ferguson, a widow in her early seventies, was a pupil at Fyvie School around 1932 when she encountered the 'Green Ladye' on the road some distance from the village.

Betty was with her chum at the time. They were walking home from school on the Aberdeen to Turriff road when a figure appeared on a gloomy stretch of the road, near Fyvie railway station. Betty told me: 'The figure of a lady in a green dress suddenly appeared on the road in front of us. It seemed to come from a wood and cross the road. It just vanished into thin air. We both saw it and got a bit of a fright. I ran home and told my mother but she said we were telling stories. But I will never forget what I saw. It is something that sticks in my mind.'

Betty's father, Alec, was a handyman at Fyvie Castle but she cannot remember him speaking about the 'Green Ladye o' Fyvie'. The legend was never mentioned, even when children of staff were entertained in the castle at Christmastime.

Fyvie School figures in a humorous legend. The day the Devil gate-crashed a classroom! The Prince of Darkness was summoned from, the depths below the earthen floor by the pupils reciting the Book of Nehemiah backwards. The schoolmaster appeared in the nick of time and persuaded the Devil to take the school cat instead of a pupil. The spot where he vanished in a puff of sulphurous flames was near an old style leading to the kirkyard. It was pointed out to wayward children by grown-ups for many years after.

Fyvie Castle, which is now in the care of The National Trust for Scotland, certainly didn't appear burdened with ghosts and curses when I visited it on a blue and gold summer day.

No phantoms lurked on the vast turnpike staircase, wide enough, it was said, for a previous laird and his chums to ride up on horseback!

There was no sign of the 'Green Ladye' in the Charter Room where one of the three Weeping Stones can be seen. Tammas the Rhymer, a 13th century seer and prophet, pronounced a curse on the lineage of Fyvie lairds after the castle gates were slammed shut in his face by a freak wind. His curse and the Weeping Stones are linked. In the past the bowl-shaped stone in the Charter Room would 'weep', filling a basin with water. One stone is believed to be built into the Preston Tower while the other is lost in the River Ythan.

In the Gordon Bedroom and Dressing Room, which is dominated by a Victorian walnut four-poster, the legend of the 'Green Ladye' lingers. I was told of a recent eerie experience of a woman who visited the room with her husband. The wife had picked up the wooden bat inscribed with details of the room when she felt as if someone was standing behind her. She thought it was a castle guide but when she turned round to speak she found herself face to face with a woman in period costume. The woman recounted the incident on a return visit and admitted Gordon blood ran in her veins!

Before leaving Fyvie I will return to the story of Dame Lilias Drummond, whose death, some claim of starvation, at Delgaty in Fife in 1601, led to the legend.

Painters carrying out work on the window frames outside the second floor Drummond Room - the chamber with the odd carving on the window sill - were astonished to look through the window and see the door open and close several times at will.

Chapter Twelve

The Phantom Smoker

Tucked amid the rolling Buchan countryside is the once thriving community of Balthangie.

In the early years of the 19th century the locals operated illicit whisky stills and smuggled brandy and other spirits landed at a small, stony beach due north of the Longmanhill, near Macduff.

The district had a school, a pub, a shop and annual attractions were the ball, held in a farm loft, and ploughing and hoeing matches.

Until the 1920s East Balthangie Farm, near Cuminestown, was part of Balthangie Estate, owned for almost a century by the Lumsden family.

Adjoining the farm today is a caravan park bearing the same name as the farm.

In February 1991, Banff and Buchan Tourist Board promoted the park's new tourist attraction. One they hoped you wouldn't meet in the dark. A resident ghost!

The pipe-smoking ghost of East Balthangie is guaranteed to attract the curious. The previous owners, Peter and Mary Crisford, and visitors to the park encountered the inexplicable aroma of pipe tobacco when there were no smokers nearby.

The smells, according to the Crisfords, were very distinct, had no obvious source and appeared to move about the park.

At least one guest claimed seeing a ghostly figure in the vicinity of the park pavilion, a green-and-white painted wooden building, which would not be out of place at an English village cricket ground.

The Crisfords investigated the mystery and came up with a theory that the park was haunted by the ghost of a farmworker who was noted for his pipe-smoking habits some 60 years ago.

The pavilion, which is a TV and recreation room, had links with the Royal Flying Corps during World War One and the ghost may be connected with flying.

While visiting the caravan park I discovered that a former laird, Harry Tailyour Lumsden was a major in the Cameron Highlanders before transferring to the Royal Flying Corps. He was killed at the age of 36 on a training flight at Brooklands. Is he the ghost of East Balthangie?

The Crisfords believed their ghost was harmless. They called him their 'friendly ghost' and grew accustomed to the signs of his presence. They even suspected the phantom was the cause of the strange behaviour of some of the equipment at the park. British Telecom was unable to explain why phones rang for no apparent reason, despite stringent tests.

The new owners at East Balthangie did not know of the alleged haunting.

But Yorkshire couple Anna and John Burdon were unshaken when I showed them the official press release put out by the tourist office.

At least it cleared up the mystery why their telephones had been acting up since they took over in April 1994. But as the next chapter reveals the Burdons had previous experience with the supernatural!

East Balthangie Farm Park is not the only caravan site in Northeast Scotland to experience a haunting.

In the early 1960s a young woman living in a residential caravan in the Aberdeen suburb of Nigg awoke to find the ghost of a Victorian lady standing in the kitchen, opposite her bedroom.

'She was wearing a grey Jane Eyre-type dress,' she told me. 'I wasn't in the least bit afraid and went back to sleep. Although I spent a very restless night, when I woke up the next morning I was neatly tucked up in bed.'

Chapter Thirteen

'The Vikings are Coming!'

'From the fury of the Northmen deliver us, O Lord.'

'T'he Vikings are coming!' The warning spread fear and terror. Bloodshed, rape and plunder followed wherever the longships of the Norsemen and the Danes landed.

The North-east neuk was not spared attack by the armies marching under the raven banner. There were rich pickings to be had over the years, culminating in the raid of 'Apardion' around 1153AD. It was the first-ever mention of Aberdeen.

Battles between Scots and the Norse invaders raged across the North-east between the ninth and twelfth centuries. After the Battle of the Bloody Pits the severed heads of three Viking kings were built into the walls of the church overlooking Gamrie Bay. Cruden Bay and Mortlach were also scenes of bloody conflict between the bitter foes.

For three years Anna and John Burdon (see previous chapter) lived in an old farm cottage on the outskirts of Maud, west of Peterhead.

Anna, a level-headed Yorkshire lass, told me the house was haunted. They used to hear the sound of voices talking from the direction of a room. Sometimes doors would open by themselves.

But nothing prepared Anna for the time she first saw the *ghost of a Viking warrior stride past her!*

It happened one night in February 1991 while she was in the bedroom. Her husband was fast asleep and she was looking out of the window.

Suddenly the solid-looking figure of the Viking appeared about 10 feet from her vantage point walking from left to right across the yard. The Viking marched in a vigorous fashion, Anna said. 'He melted into the wall of the steading and I did not see him again that night,' she added.

She gave me a graphic description of the phantom. He wore a brownish tabard, a mucky cream undershirt, a kilt or skirt-like garment to his knees. She did not see footwear or leggings because his legs 'vanished' when he reached a pile of stones near the steading.

58

On his head was a helmet 'resembling an upturned egg' - contrary to popular belief Vikings did not wear horned headgear. He had long blonde hair and a beard. He was carrying a round shield but she did not notice a sword or battleaxe in his possession. The vision lasted only a matter of seconds.

Anna saw the Viking ghost on one more occasion. A few weeks later she was exercising her dogs at night when she saw him about 10 yards from her. This time she was standing beside a gate to a field when he materialized. Electric light from a shed unit lit up the scene. The Viking took exactly the same route as before, except Anna watched his progress from a different angle. He marched from right to left and again the ghost vanished into the steading wall.

'The figure was not malevolent,' said Anna. 'He was marching along in a business-like manner. He didn't make a sound and didn't seem to notice me.'

The phantom was not Anna's first brush with the spectral world. The Burdons lived in a house in Bradford, which became subject to hauntings after a sealed room was unlocked. It was as if a time capsule had been opened. The room contained old gaslight fixtures, brass curtain rods and rings and Victorian wallpaper. A 'grey shadow' and a 'cold spot' on the stairs proved frightening, particularly to the dog.

But what was behind the bizarre sighting of the Viking ghost? What incident was re-enacted from the past?

Was the warrior part of a raiding party making tracks for his longship? The Abbey of Deer was built a century after the last Viking raid in North-east Scotland, but there was still booty to be had in other religious establishments.

Was he fleeing the scene of a battle? Why not the Battle of the Bloody Butts? It was fought at Lendrum, near Turriff, less than 10 miles south-west from where Anna Burdon saw the ghost.

Aberdeen Daily Journal photo of the Gordon Place 'haunted'
house in January 1920.
(Courtesy: Aberdeen City Arts & Recreation Libraries Division).

The Red Well, Whitehills. On New Year's Day 1990 a phantom
confronted a teenager near this spot.

The Ghost of Red Well Road pursued Christopher Christie
across the playing field (left).

61

Druminnor Castle, where the Gordons were slaughtered by their Clan Forbes hosts in the 16th century.

A group of friends were accompanied by the 'Green Witch' on this stretch of the Slug Road, near Stonehaven.

High Spirits: Mysterious rapping has been heard in Cameron's Inn, Aberdeen.

An archaeologist unearths a grave during the Carmelite Friary 'dig' at The Green, Aberdeen. (Photo courtesy: Aberdeen Art Gallery and Museums Collections).

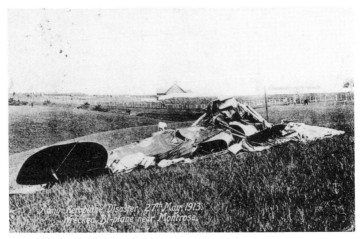

Wreck of Lt Desmond Arthur's plane at Lunan Bay in May
1913. (Photo courtesy: Montrose Aerodrome Museum Society).

Waldron Road Bridge. Ian McIntosh stands at the spot where
the Montrose Ghost was seen during the last war.

Anna Burdon at the front door of the pavilion at haunted East Balthangie Farm Caravan Park.

The 'Green Ladye o' Fyvie' is said to stalk the vast turnpike stair at Fyvie Castle.

Hallgreen Castle, Inverbervie, is the haunt of ghostly figures, weird sounds - and 'The Watcher'.

The eerie effigy of 'The Watcher' guards a corridor in Hallgreen Castle.

The ghosts of Craigievar were invited to the wedding of the Hon.
Kirstine Forbes-Sempill and John Cable in June 1968.

The haunted Blue Room at Craigievar Castle is in the corbelled turret (right, lower windows).

Kingcausie, Maryculter, photographed in 1910. The patter of ghostly feet were heard in a corridor.
(Photo courtesy: J.W. Irvine-Fortescue).

A ghost known as 'Mary' walked Deeford in Riverside Drive, Aberdeen.

The Mercat Cross, Aberdeen. The Laird of Leith Hall was shot dead in a quarrel near here in 1763.

Leith Hall, Aberdeenshire. Author Elizabeth Byrd wrote about its ghosts.

The Ninian Southern oil production platform.
(Photo courtesy: Chevron UK Ltd).

The Lecht Phantom: Old photograph of 'Toplis Cottage'.

Wullie Wright at the time of the Lecht haunting.
(Photo courtesy: David Wright).

Chapter Fourteen

'The Watcher'

Aspectre dubbed 'The Watcher' by Baron Brigfoord is the most sinister of the ghostly company that haunts Hallgreen Castle, a red-sandstone laird's house overlooking Bervie Bay.

On my visit I bumped into the tall figure of 'The Watcher' in a narrow corridor. His pale face stared at me from under a black hood. But this particular Watcher was only an effigy, dressed to give castle guests, and, perhaps future tourists, a thrill.

Baron Brigfoord - Yorkshireman Ian McMillan - assured me that the actual ghost had a far more chilling affect on him. Ian was working in the long corridor one day when the hairs on his neck prickled. He turned to see a cloaked figure behind him. It was 'The Watcher'.

As we chatted in his study, one of 33 rooms in Hallgreen, he told me: 'The Watcher is the only one of the castle ghosts who gives the impression he would do you some harm. When you see him coming you get out of his way.'

He described 'The Watcher' as being tall, well-built and cloaked from head to foot. So far, he has been unable to distinguish his face.

His wife Helen and their five young sons have all caught glimpses of the phantom - Helen actually saw the sinister figure reflected in a mirror.

Explained Ian: 'We call him The Watcher because he appears to be standing guard over the old cells where prisoners were kept. We think he may have watched over them.'

The McMillans first set eyes on Hallgreen while castle-hunting in Scotland in 1983. They were faced with a monumental task of restoring the castle, the shell of a Victorian building around the nucleus of a 14th century stronghold. It had no staircases, no floors, no roof and no electricity or water.

For eight years Helen brought up the boys in a caravan in the cobbled courtyard and also helped Ian make the castle habitable.

Antique dealer Ian restored the castle flagstone by flagstone and turret by turret. Original oak beams dating back to 1374 were refurbished. The huge fireplace in the Great Hall, which burns a ton of wood in a single night, was brought back to its former glory. A secret passage and staircase leading from the dungeon to the great hall was uncovered.

The family's first brush with the unknown took place while mum and dad were out. The children's baby-sitter phoned and asked the couple to come home. The caravan was being shaken and the lights were going on and off.

Ian's first encounter took place while he was excavating a corridor that had collapsed. He stepped outside a door to have a coffee and a cigarette and to admire the view when he was aware of two men standing at his elbow. *They were wearing body armour!*

Ian told me: 'They were very rough-looking characters. I think they were both bare-headed but one might have had a beard. They could have been dressed in kilts, but I am not sure. We didn't speak - we were just three people looking out across the bay. When I looked again they had vanished, I've never seen them since.'

In the early days of their occupancy the McMillans experienced a malevolent atmosphere in their new home, culminating in what Helen calls the 'Castle of Blood' incident.

One Saturday afternoon in 1985, as Ian worked in the corridor, Helen was changing five-month-old Jonathan's nappy in their temporary bedroom in the guest wing. When she left the baby for a minute to go into the adjoining bathroom he was happily kicking his legs on his parents' bed.

Helen told me: 'When I came back I was horrified to see blood everywhere - on the bed clothes and bedside furniture and on Jonathan. He was covered from head to foot, yet I knew he was unharmed for he was giggling and smiling.

'It wasn't even fresh blood. It was thick, congealed. We wrapped him in a towel and took him to the Health Centre where a doctor cleaned him up. There were no cuts or wounds on my baby - nothing.' According to Helen the doctor wrote 'Unexplained' on the report.

Helen told me about another frightening experience when she was chased at night from the Great Hall by a white figure. 'It looked like a traditional ghost', she explained. 'At first I thought it was a trick of light until it moved, then it moved towards me.' Helen fled.

Other manifestations at Hallgreen have included mysterious noises, the ghost of a Victorian woman, wearing a green laced dress with a little girl, and the crying of a baby.

It's not just the McMillan family who have seen strange things.

Two couples were invited for dinner and as the evening progressed it was decided to hold a seance. Ian and Helen and their guests gathered in the small, vaulted 14th century kitchen. It was winter time and the room was heated with electric fires and gas heaters and candles were burning.

Suddenly the atmosphere grew cold, and within seconds it was freezing. It was then two ghostly servant girls walked in. Ian told me: 'One girl was older than the other. They were dressed in coarse material and wearing simple linen shifts.'

Not everyone saw the apparitions but one of the guests started talking to them.

On another occasion a guest, a level-headed insurance broker from London, quit the Queen's Bedroom and spent the rest of the night on a settee in the TV lounge. He had been frightened by a strange woman who had stood at his bedside. The room is said to be haunted by a woman who committed suicide after the death of her child.

Experts on ghostly phenomena have been baffled by the events. One woman psychic collapsed near the old wells claiming the remains of a child lies at the bottom. She wants the body exhumed.

If Hallgreen Castle had a violent past there are no clues to be found in the history books.

The earlier part of the castle was erected by the Dunnets, and in time it passed through a great number of owners, including the Raits, Coutts the bankers, the Barclays of Urie, and so on. During the French Revolutionary War of 1800 the Provost of Inverbervie hoodwinked a French privateer into thinking the castle's battlements were bristling with cannon and the would-be invasion was repelled without bloodshed.

But horror lingers elsewhere in the neighbourhood. One of Scotland's most fiendish crimes took place two miles from Inverbervie.

A hollow by a stream at Browniesleys Farm is known as the Sheriff's Kettle, and, according to tradition, it marks the spot where in the 15th century the unpopular Sheriff of the Mearns was murdered by local barons and hell broth made from his flesh and bones!

Chapter Fifteen

The Delgatie Mystery

For seven centuries a castle of the Hays of Erroll has stood at Delgatie, where a local farm is equally famous for its barnyards celebrated in a popular bothy ballad.

The Hays were famed for their warlike qualities. Indeed, their very name is Gaelic for 'wall', given to three heroic Hays after they stood firm against invading Danes at the Battle of Luncarty. King Robert the Bruce rewarded the Clan Chief with the title of Hereditary Lord High Constable of Scotland for his loyalty during the Scottish War of Independence.

Two hundred years later the Hays were virtually decimated at Flodden. And after the Battle of Glenlivet in 1594 Delgatie Castle was badly damaged after a long siege. The exiled Hays were only allowed to return to the great house on agreeing they would keep the peace and that no new walls more than an arrow-shaft thick would be erected.

In the following century Sir William Hay of Delgatie fought alongside the Duke of Montrose. After the ill-fated battle of Carbisdale he was captured and hanged with his master in Edinburgh in May 1650. Their bodies were buried next to each other in St Giles Cathedral.

So it is appropriate 'The Delgatie Mystery' should occur when the country was again threatened by war, and the 16th century stronghold, the third castle to be built at Delgatie, was occupied by the military.

The present laird, Captain John Hay of Delgatie, told me of two strange occurrences which took place while troops were billeted in the castle from 1940 to 1945.

On two, dreich nights within a year the small garrison hastily collected their weapons and fled outside. As the troops, some in barefeet, waited in the darkness a search was made of the five-storey towerhouse to establish the cause of inexplicable noises that had upset so many soldiers.

The castle, which is two miles east of Turriff, was handed back by the military after the war. But so far Captain Hay has been unable to solve the mystery.

In 1994 he spoke to a former sapper who had been at Delgatie. He too had heard of the strange occurrences, but laughed them off. Both British and foreign troops were stationed in the castle during the war years.

So is the castle haunted? Captain Hay has never seen or heard any phantoms but he told me: 'People always think that ghosts are malevolent - but if the castle is haunted then our ghosts are benevolent. You never feel lonely - the castle has such a friendly atmosphere.'

Chapter Sixteen

'The Ghost Man'

Who's Who listed his hobbies as: 'walking and ghost hunting.' Elliott O'Donnell's love of ghostlore began in the Victorian era and carried on till his death in 1965, at the grand old age of 93!

During an active career O'Donnell ranched in the United States, turned to acting in England, then became an author, with 50 books and magazine and newspaper articles, mostly about the supernatural, to his name. It earned him the soubriquet, 'The Ghost Man'.

He was never far from controversy. In 1922 he created a sensation in the United States and Britain by disclosing an Anti-Male Movement among 'ultra-feminists' in London.

O'Donnell was born in County Limerick, Ireland, in 1872, the youngest son of a Church of England country vicar.

His search for ghosts took him all over the country, and around the turn of the century he visited friends in Aberdeen, where he had first-hand experience of ghostly phenomena.

He stayed at their home in the vicinity of Provost Ross's House in the Shiprow, and, had barely climbed into bed when he heard a noise coming from the direction of a window recess.

In the moonlight he saw something rise from the floor of the room and glide towards him. He sensed danger, with good reason. For the thing suddenly attacked him, seizing him by the throat and forcing him on his pillow. O'Donnell struggled in vain as the grip on his throat tightened. He blacked out, and when he came to he was alone in the dark room. At dawn he examined the room. He had locked the door himself the previous night and the windows were securely bolted!

At breakfast his hosts owned up. They admitted they had deliberately lodged him in the room because they suspected it was haunted and they knew O'Donnell had psychic powers.

It transpired that in the middle of the 19th century the room had been part of a private home for mentally-disturbed people from wealthy families, and that a patient or nurse had been killed in the room.

O'Donnell slept with one eye open during the rest of his stay at the house.

A few days later the ghosthunter came across another haunted house - in Schoolhill. A 'To Let' notice hung in the window and he and friends decided to hold a night vigil.

One of the ghostwatchers was a girl who had worked in the house as a maid. She claimed she had seen the ghost on two occasions. According to her story the phantom was the cause of breaking up the family and cost the girl her job.

While lodged at the house the girl said she was kept awake by strange noises, a pale light, and the touch of something cold and damp stroking her cheeks.

O'Donnell and his fellow ghosthunters were rewarded for their long vigil. A pale light materialized on the plaster wall of the room - followed by a bizarre, white face of a woman. The hatched-shaped features were framed with black hair neatly parted down the muddle, and hanging in loops over the ears.

But the face had no eyes and no sockets!

As the terrifying features melted into the wall a door slammed in the basement corridor. O'Donnell was first out of the room and was in time to see a woman disappear through a closed door at the end of the corridor. When O'Donnell and other witnesses entered this room they saw the apparition kneeling on the stone-flagged floor. Even as she attempted to lift a flagstone the figure vanished.

Inquiries by 'The Ghost Man' revealed a strange story. A woman had murdered her husband and child in order to remarry. But she was struck down by smallpox before she could do so. She became blind and eventually took her life. O'Donnell discovered the bodies had been hidden in the room where he and his fellow ghosthunters had seen the phantom disappear.

There was an equally chilling climax to a chapter in O'Donnell's book, *Scottish Ghost Stories* (1911), concerning a haunted house in the neighbourhood of Great Western Road, Aberdeen.

A certain Mr Scarfe was accompanied by his dog on the ghostwatch. Both man and dog were terrified at what followed. A strange phosphorescent glow in a passage heralded the arrival of the phantom - a middle-aged woman with a startlingly white face, straight nose, and prominent front teeth. The creeping ghost motioned Scarfe to follow her up a staircase. The cold, grey dawn met them as they entered a garret, where, after pointing downwards at the hearth, the woman suddenly vanished.

The landlord was summoned and on investigation a stamped and addressed envelope was found under the floorboards.

Investigations showed that the letter, containing a postal order, had vanished during the time the house was occupied by a family named Piblington, and that their maid, Anna Webb, whose description fitted that of the ghost, was accused of theft. The poor woman hanged herself in the cellar, unaware that the letter had somehow slipped through a crack in the floor.

Another of O'Donnell's Aberdeen stories took place in the White Dove Hotel, somewhere near St Swithin's Street, and tells how the ghost of a Hindu child, its throat horribly slashed, kept watch over a dying woman.

During his stay in Aberdeen the master of the macabre refuted local stories that the Trinity Hall in Union Street was haunted by the ghost of a decorator, and that phantom footsteps were heard in the Music Hall.

But O'Donnell, who loved animals, confirmed that houses, latterly offices, near the Joint Station were haunted by a phantom dog.

Chapter Seventeen

Sleepless in Craigievar

As I mingled with wedding guests on the lawn, bagpipe music floated above the fairy-tale skyline of corbelled turrets and crow-stepped gables of Craigievar Castle.

The bride wore a silk taffeta gown in Forbes dress tartan. On her head sparkled a tiara, and a lace veil worn by her great, great-grandmother.

There was a tinge of disappointment in the summer air. The surprise guests had failed to show face. Probably just as well. For the white invitation card displayed on the ornate mantelpiece in the Great Hall was addressed to the bride's ancestral ghosts. All ten of them!

The newly-weds had particularly wanted an appearance by the second baronet, 'Red' Sir John Forbes (1636-1703), so called because of his complexion and fiery temper. But we had to settle for his likeness which beamed approval from his portrait in the Tartan Bedroom.

The date was Saturday, 1 June 1968. The occasion: The marriage of the Hon. Kirstine Forbes-Sempill and London chartered accountant John Cable. After the ceremony some 170 guests attended the reception in a marquee on the castle lawn.

Why didn't 'Red' Sir John and his fellow spectres fail to acknowledge the invitation? 'Too many people about,' smiled the newly-weds.

The ghosts of Craigievar needed no second bidding on less auspicious occasions.

Ghostly phenomena has been detected by a number of persons in different parts of the castle, which is seven storeys high, including its porch tower. At one time there was a haunted well under the floor of the kitchen in the barrel-vaulted basement which also consisted of the cellars and dungeons. A fiddler is reported to have been drowned in the well. The legend gave rise to the rhyme:

If you sit there on a windy day,
You'll hear the fiddler begin to play!

It has been suggested his wraith glides silently through the castle at night, opening and shutting doors and who will only appear to those persons bearing the name of Forbes!

The castle and its lands were bought in the year 1610 by an Aberdeen merchant William Forbes - nicknamed 'Danzig Willie' because he had made 'a goodlie pile in the Danzig trade.'

But Craigievar's most notorious laird was 'Red' Sir John Forbes, whose clan were traditional feudal enemies of the Gordons. He is said to have forced a Gordon at sword-point through the narrow window of the Blue Room, so that the intruder plunged four storeys to his death.

The aperture was bricked up, but when The National Trust for Scotland took the castle into their care in 1963 the window was reopened.

The Blue Room is said to be haunted. Cecilia, Lady Sempill, the last of the family to live in the castle, often slept in the room, and one night reported a 'strange presence.'

Undaunted by tales of haunted Craigievar, Ken Adams, who was then editor of the weekly newspaper, *The Deeside Piper*, decided to spend the night alone in the castle in the dead of a Scottish winter!

A few days before Christmas 1986, Ken turned up at the castle, situated in the secluded glen of the Leochel Burn, 26 miles west of Aberdeen.

He was given a candlelit 'spook's tour' by the housekeeper, Mrs Frances Scott. A strong westerly wind swept round the castle walls as he was led into the Great Hall, its furnishings protected by white sheets. 'I was reminded of the haunted house film when a sheet rises eerily into the air,' recalled Ken, 'but I wasn't laughing at the time.'

Ken was told that the magnificent hall was the scene of weird happenings. Lady Sempill had claimed 'encountering a crowd of ghosts' in the hall during a visit by her solicitor.

Until the middle of the 18th century, Barony Courts sat in the Great Hall. In bygone times the laird had the power of 'pit and gallows'. The surviving court books tell their own story. One tenant was fined £100 for slandering his wife and mother. He accused them of witchcraft. Beating, blood-spilling and wounding were common complaints.

The Blue Room, where Ken decided to spend the night, is said to take its name from the blue-coloured hangings woven by a laird's wife.

At 10pm Mrs Scott, who lived in a cottage in the grounds, said her farewells. Because of the fire risk Ken was not allowed a naked flame during his vigil. He had to settle for a flashlight instead.

A few minutes later he was snug in his sleeping bag. But he found it near impossible to sleep. The wind howled furiously and rain tapped wildly on the window panes.

Suddenly, he shot bolt upright. Footsteps were rapidly ascending the stairs outside the Blue Room! 'I experienced abject terror - and had a vision of escaping through the window.' But Ken's late night visitor was no ghost. His photographer had left a piece of equipment behind and had roused Mrs Scott to gain an unscheduled entry.

But Ken Adams did experience something unusual during his stay.

He detected the strong smell of burning peat in his room. It had been years since the fuel was used to heat the castle. Ken told me: 'The smell got stronger and stronger. I shone my torch at the foot of the door but there was no sign of smoke. After a short time the smell disappeared altogether.'

Ken eventually drifted into an uneasy sleep, no doubt pondering Red Sir John's personal motto: 'Do not vaiken sleiping dogs!'

When I revisited creaky old Craigievar it was hard to believe 26 years had elapsed since the fairy-tale wedding. Did the couple really invite the castle ghosts?

The proof is there for all to see. The invitation card, marked 'The Ghosts of Craigievar', is still propped against the mantelpiece shelf.

My National Trust guide sounded dubious about the hauntings but he did tell me of a strange incident when a man who dared spend the night in the castle alone heard footsteps on the stairs - but when he checked there was no one there! Now where had I heard that one before?

Chapter Eighteen

To the Manor Haunted

I gazed into the deep stairwell at Kingcausie and pondered the terrible tragedy that had overtaken a small boy and his grieving family in the Deeside mansion shortly before Christmas 1836.

James Turner Christie was 22 months old when they visited the great house at Maryculter.

During their stay the child pestered his nanny to lift him up to peer over the top banister - but he wriggled free and plunged 30 feet to his death.

Today James sleeps beneath tall pines in the nearby ruined Templar kirkyard by the River Dee.

But one night in 1962 his footsteps were heard pattering along the topmost corridor at Kingcausie!

James William Irvine-Fortescue, the present and 15th laird of Kingcausie - pronounced 'Kincowsie' - and his wife Margaret shared the uncanny experience.

After we had climbed the 39 steps to visit the scene of the haunting, Mr Irvine-Fortescue told me: 'We would leave our bedroom door open at night in case our littlest son, Jamie should come to us.'

'On this particular night, it was about 3am, we were wakened by a pattering of feet of a child running past our door. I lay in bed while Margaret went to find Jamie. But he and our other two children were safely tucked up in bed fast asleep. We heard the pattering on several other occasions when there were no children in the house.'

The laird told me of another strange incident which occurred in 1952 when his father came down for breakfast one morning. 'Did you hear that loud knocking on my door in the night?' he asked the assembled family. 'It went like this'. He demonstrated the sound by banging so violently on the table for a few moments 'that the plates danced.'

Mr Irvine-Fortescue told me: 'I remember asking my father why we hadn't seen or heard the family ghost recently.' His father replied: 'What do you expect in a house full of agnostics!'

The present laird's mother, Ruth, lived alone at Kingcausie

during the last war. She told him that every night she took her courage in both hands before she could face going up to bed alone - in the haunted room!

'The Chinese Room', so called because of its Oriental furnishings, is on the same floor as the haunted corridor. It has been given a sinister reputation by some writers. In the last century when Anne, 12th Lady Kingcausie (1826-1909), reported a strange happening to the housekeeper the old woman told her 'nae to fash hersel aboot sic affairs, but that there were things aboot that room which were better nae told aboot.'

Said the 15th laird: 'My mother was deeply religious and always placed a copy of the Bible on her bedside table to keep away the ghosts.'

An uncle, Lt-Col. William Prenville Irvine-Fortescue, claimed 'The Chinese Room' had 'evil influences'. On the two occasions he slept there his bedclothes were lifted high into the air before sinking to the floor.

'He said he was absolutely terrified,' recalled Mr Irvine-Fortescue. 'I've never slept in 'The Chinese Room', but I don't think there is anything evil about the room.'

When the sisters of the present laird's grandfather slept in the room when very young they too were frightened when the bedclothes rose into the air before sliding on to the floor.

Mr Irvine-Fortescue may not have seen a ghost at Kingcausie - but it was a different story when as a child he lived at Eastland, a 250-year-old house on the estate.

He was only four at the time. At breakfast one morning he told his mother: 'Such a funny little brown man came and looked at me in bed. He just smiled and went away!'

In 1920 when another family was living at Eastland a girl said one day: 'Oh, mummy, mummy - there's a little monkey in the corner of my room.'

It transpired she meant 'a little monk!'

In the 1930s Mr Irvine-Fortescue's mother gave two elderly ladies a lift in her car at Milltimber Brae. On discovering that they had lived at Eastland in the 1890s the conversation turned to ghosts. They volunteered information that the house had been haunted by a little monk who smiled as they passed on the stairs!

The ghost is believed to be that of a Catholic priest who held Mass in the house during the time it was owned by the Menzies family.

Turreted Kingcausie, which was begun by the first laird, Henry Irvine, in the 15th century, isn't the only North-east mansion with a haunted reputation.

In 1688, Thomas Burnett, the second son of James Burnett of Craigmyle, purchased Kemnay House and its surrounding lands.

The Burnetts have been there ever since. In 1964, Mrs Susan Milton, a direct descendant of the first Burnett to own the house, arrived with her family from South Africa.

The new owner of Kemnay House - the oldest parts of the building may date from the late 15th century - found that a bedroom and the main staircase were supposed to be haunted.

Tradition has it that in the 18th century, during the time of George Burnett of Kemnay, an employee called Morrison - some versions of the story say he was the factor - hanged himself in the small room, which is still known as 'Morrison's Room'.

The reason for the suicide is obscure. The most popular explanation is that he was involved in a murder in the room, while another version tells of a pregnant servant girl, whom he jilted.

On the anniversary of the double tragedy Morrison's ghost is said to appear in the room after climbing the left-handed staircase which spirals through the centre of the house.

Mrs Milton believes the ghost story and its origins have been somewhat embellished down through the years. She told me that neither she nor any members of her family had seen or heard the ghost, although a great-aunt Amelia would sometimes sit up until the dead of night in the hope of meeting the phantom!

But there is a germ of truth in the story. While family papers were being researched it was found that a man called Morrison did work for the laird George Burnett. It seems Morrison blotted his copybook by neglecting his duties, resulting in cattle straying into the house.

The picturesque Aberdeenshire mansion of Westhall, which stands close to where the Gadie runs and has imposing views of Bennachie, is also reputed to be haunted.

There is no record of the date on which the original house was built or by whom, but its keep has its roots in the 11th century. Westhall is mentioned as a seat belonging to the church and diocese of Aberdeen as early as the 13th century.

After the Reformation the lands of Westhall, Ryehill, Pitmedden, Ardoyne, Old Rayne, Pitmachie and others were acquired by James Horn, vicar of Elgin.

The oldest walls of the three-storey mansion are about five feet thick, and very strong. In the last century considerable additions were made to the building by Lady Leith, widow of General Alexander of Freefield.

The ghost of Westhall is said to be a 'Green Lady', daughter of a previous owner who hurled herself from a window in the keep.

Cullen House, built on a high rock overlooking the Burn of Cullen on the Moray Firth, is the former seat of the Seafield family.

The 16th century mansion, which was converted into flats in the 1980s, is reputed to be haunted by the ghost of the 'Mad Earl' - the third Earl of Seafield, who is supposed to have murdered his factor in November 1770, and then in remorse committed suicide.

But after spending a week-end at Cullen House in the summer of 1963, clairvoyant Tom Corbett, claimed he had come across two resident phantoms.

Mr Corbett said while investigating the hauntings he saw the same ghost in the library and on a landing at the top of the Pink Staircase. Was it the 'Mad Earl'? Mr Corbett could not be positive. The figure did not appear to be dressed in clothes of the period nor anything so elaborate as the third Earl wears in a portrait. The ghosthunter was reticent about the second ghost.

And he assured his hostess, the Countess of Seafield, that there was 'no cause for fear.' The ghost could not be described as an unhappy one.' So that would appear to rule out the 'Mad Earl'!

Mr Corbett had an amusing anecdote for reporters when he spoke to them at Cullen. He repeated a conversation he had overheard between two women visitors on the haunted staircase during the hours part of the house was open to the public.

'I heard one woman, who did not know who I was, say to another that there ought to be a ghost. And you know, she was actually standing just where I saw the ghost.'

Apart from Tom Corbett the ghost of Cullen House was reputed to have been seen by a number of people over the years, including the late Countess of Seafield herself, house guests, a maid and two journalists.

After the Battle of Barra, near Oldmeldrum, on Ascension Day 1308, the victorious Robert the Bruce rewarded an Aberdeen burgess family, the Strabroks, with the lands of Foveran on the Ythan estuary.

Thirty years later, in the reign of King David II, the barony of

Foveran was relinquished in favour of William de Turin or Turing, who built a castle, incorporating its famous Turing Tower, overlooking the sand dunes and the North Sea.

But during the Civil War, John, the 13th laird of Turing, fought under the banner of King Charles I, and forfeited his estates as a result.

During the 18th century Foveran House was built by John Robertson of Pitmillan, a merchant and former Provost of Aberdeen. It was erected no great distance from the old castle, using much of the stones for the new property.

After occupying Foveran for 99 years John Robertson's grandson sold the estate piecemeal and the mansion and policies were acquired by the Mackenzie family

The last resident laird of Foveran was a woman - the reclusive Florence Mary Mackenzie, who succeeded her father, Major-General Roderick Mackenzie of Kintail and Seaforth.

It is her ghost that is said to haunt the great house.

North-east author David Toulmin, who lived in the parish for 21 years, recalled years later how the old lady kept marauding schoolboys away from her apple orchard with the aid of a double-barrelled shotgun loaded with barley!

He wrote: 'Living severely alone in Foveran House hemmed in on all sides by the densely wooded policies, Miss Mackenzie became something of a bird in a gilded cage; a Lady of Shalott in her ivory tower, isolated and almost feared by her indifference to strangers, so that very few people intruded upon her serene privacy.

'What it was like for an old lady living alone in the vast mansion is difficult to imagine, what with its ghostly cellars and subterranean stone passages, dark forbidding kitchens with their prison-bar windows; turreted stairways, labyrinthine pillared alcoves and piano-key ceilings, marble fireplaces and walls in velvet textured paper - these were for the style and pomp of a former aristocracy - latterly the reclusion of a lonely old spinster, companion of the cellar rats and bats of the Turing Tower, the rookeries of spring her liveliest season, but perhaps she enjoyed her independence.'

By 1953 Miss Mackenzie had installed bathrooms on every landing and electricity. 'She had every modern convenience,' wrote Toulmin, 'plus a personal courage that was a challenge to anyone in the whole parish to sleep alone for a night in Foveran House.'

Miss Mackenzie died at Foveran in June 1973, at the age of 94.

In 1982 Foveran House took on a new lease of life and today it is a comfortable country house hotel.

But there have been reports of apparent psychic phenomena in recent years. Residents have reported seeing an apparition.

One of the dogs belonging to the management 'sensed' something strange and has on occasions refused to go upstairs.

The most mysterious happening took place around midnight on a calm night when two members of management were working in the bar area, after locking up. Suddenly the locked door of the original ballroom began to rattle and shake. So fierce was the shaking that the door came off its hinges! The door was unlocked. The room was found to be empty and silent.

Royal Deeside's baronial-style Ardoe House is reputed to be haunted by a White Lady.

The ghost of Katherine Ogston is said to stalk the staircase of the country house hotel. Staff and guests have felt her presence over the years.

Entertainer Tommy Steele has claimed he saw the ghost while staying at the hotel during his Scottish pop tour in 1958.

In 1990 a taxi driver who arrived to collect his passenger early one morning was startled to see a mystery woman in a nightdress descend the stairs. The figure melted away.

Katherine was the wife of a previous laird, Alexander Milne Ogston, whose family bought Ardoe House and its estate in 1839. The Ogstons were descended from Norman stock, and made their fortune manufacturing soap and candles in their Aberdeen factory, hence their nickname, the 'Soapy' Ogstons.

Further along the South Deeside Road historic Maryculter House Hotel, which was part of the manor house of the Knights Templar and their successors, the Knights of St John of Jerusalem, is also reported to be haunted by a phantom lady.

A Regency mansion in the Ferryhill district of Aberdeen is haunted by the *upper half of a ghost!*

Devanha House was originally built in 1813, but was extended by the famous city architect Archibald Simpson in 1840, probably following a fire.

The building provides accommodation for employees of an oil-related company. In recent years both guests and staff have reported seeing the ghost of an elderly grey-haired lady, from the waist upwards, roaming the house at various times of the day.

The ghost, which is described as 'warm and friendly', has been seen in various bedrooms and in a lounge. Some witnesses say they have sensed the ghost before actually seeing it.

Her dress sense sounds interesting. Of the several persons who have met the spectre their descriptions of her dress have tallied. It resembled a 'white, baggy T-shirt!', I was told. Perhaps the ghost was wearing night attire, or a shroud!

The Devanha House Ghost may have been associated with the mansion from its earliest days, which might explain why only half a ghost is seen. Old historic buildings undergo structural changes through time and that's why some spectres appear to walk through doors and walls which did not exist in their lifetime. When the level of flooring has been raised the ghost materializes from the ankles and knees upwards. If Devanha House was damaged by fire in the early 19th century it is possible Archibald Simpson carried out extensive alterations.

Chapter Nineteen

Holy Ghosts

The Earl of Buchan chose the valley between Sapling Brae and Aikey Brae, the latter once famous for its horse fair, to build the Abbey of St Mary of Deer in the early years of the 13th century.

The small, cruciform church stood virtually untouched until the last century when the eccentric Admiral Ferguson, who, it was rumoured, kept pet alligators in the Temple of Theseus at Pitfour Loch, utilized the stone for building purposes on his vast estate.

The A950 - the Peterhead to New Pitsligo road - runs past the arched ruins of the Cistercian Abbey of Deer.

It was on this road one night in 1929 that a young couple out walking saw the ghost of a monk!

Mrs Margaret Robertson, who now lives in Fraserburgh, was a teenager when she saw the phantom.

She and her friend had set out from the village of Mintlaw and had reached the low stone parapet of a bridge where a burn runs beneath the road into a wood, opposite present-day Saplinbrae House Hotel.

It was a moonless night but quite starry and they could see a short distance. As the couple sat on the parapet talking 'there was a swishing noise like a breeze blowing through the trees.'

Margaret recalled: 'On the middle of the road there appeared the form of a very tall man.

'As he walked past us, you could see he was dressed in a long dark coat or cloak, with either a hood or shawl on his head with a white strip from his neck down the front.

'His face was just a grey blur but you could see the feet, which looked very large, as this form walked past without any noise. It was a shadowy figure.

'We both watched till it disappeared in the dark.'

Margaret turned to her companion: 'What on earth was that?' she asked. 'We were very afraid,' she told me.

Moments later a motor car rounded the bend of the road beside the abbey a short distance further on. The vehicle's headlamps swept the road but there was no sign of the mysterious figure. The road was deserted.

'I believe the tall man was dressed the way the monks in the abbey dressed. I never did sit on that bridge again and when I went past the spot on my bike I pedalled very fast!'

Said Margaret: 'Since that night I never dismiss stories of seeing an apparition or a ghostly figure.'

Margaret and her companion were not the only persons to see something strange on the A950.

Soon after the incident she spoke to a cyclist who swerved violently one night to avoid colliding with a 'huge black thing' on the highway. 'By God,' the man told her, 'I didn't half put a spurt on after that!'

Hauntings ecclesiastic are well documented throughout the country. Cathedrals, abbeys, nunneries, kirks and graveyards have their own ghost story. The 'Haunted Neuk' is no different.

The ghostly monk of Deer Abbey reminds me of a similar apparition seen in an Aberdeen house!

I was told the story in Christmas 1960 when, as a reporter with the *Scottish Daily Record*, I was asked to host a luncheon party for local old age pensioners in the Douglas Hotel, Aberdeen. After the meal table talk turned to a favourite subject at Yuletide - ghosts!

One old lady startled us by announcing: 'I've seen a ghost!'. She told us how, as a young country lass, she had moved to Aberdeen to work in a shop.

Her first night was spent in lodgings in Wales Street, in the East End of the city. Despite the strange surroundings she fell asleep immediately. But during the night she awoke with a start to find a weird, hooded figure at the foot of the bed. The apparition resembled a monk from the past. 'It didn't have a face, and didn't make a sound,' the old lady told her engrossed audience. Terrified, the young girl gave a strangled cry. At that moment the monk glided towards the bedroom wall - and vanished!

In bygone times Aberdeen had several religious orders - the Grey Friars, Black Friars, White Friars and Red Friars - but none of their monasteries were situated in the vicinity of Wales Street. The Knights Templar, a religious military order, did own land not too far away - in the Market Stance, off Justice Street. Was there a connection?

One of the earliest documented hauntings concerning church property occurred in Old Aberdeen in the 16th century.

William Orem, the Town Clerk of Old Aberdeen, mentioned the

ghost in his description of life in the burgh during the years of 1724 and 1725

Before the Reformation a number of prebendary manses on land around St Machar's Cathedral was occupied by parsons representing various parishes throughout the North-east.

Orem noted that the Clatt manse was 'called Tam Framper's house because it was haunted.' The local populace had probably given the house this puzzling soubriquet soon after it was abandoned.

Historian Katherine E. Trail, who was brought up in Old Aberdeen and whose father, Professor Milligan, was the first to occupy the Chair of Biblical Criticism at King's College, wrote in 1929 that the name was 'not suggestive of a high-class ghost!'. A certain George Cruickshank inherited the former Clatt manse, only to use the stones to build a salmon bothy at the Bridge of Don.

The rest of the material from the haunted house and other Old Aberdeen properties, including the Bishop's Palace, was used by Cromwell's Roundheads to build a fort at Castlehill when they occupied Aberdeen in 1651. But such desecration did not go unpunished. While workmen were removing dressed sandstone lining a well in the palace courtyard the walls collapsed on top of them. But the Roundheads took such adversity in their stride, for the fort was built, and traces of its walls can still be seen at Castlehill.

Old Aberdeen's Chaplains Court, built by Bishop Dunbar in 1519, is the oldest inhabited house in the city.

Twenty or more chaplains from nearby St Machar's Cathedral lived there, having a common table, and I was interested to hear that on one occasion a former occupant saw a ghostly, but sociable, company of men in old-fashioned dress gathered round a table.

Novelist Agnes Short, who lived there with her family for 20 years, heard the story from a previous householder.

One evening Mrs Short reported seeing the indistinct shape of a woman walk across a bedroom - but apart from sensing a benign presence on other occasions the family saw nothing else during their stay. 'It is a very happy house,' said Mrs Short of her former home.

Over the years the Shorts heard of various 'hauntings' from others - a woman doing needlework, phantom footsteps and the ghostly rustling of a skirt in a corridor.

Agnes Short was recently asked about the ghost of a small girl seen in the garden - a tale invented by her daughter when very young!

A secret underground passage was said to run from the house to the Bishop's Palace and the Cathedral.

The ghost of a clergyman was encountered in a manse in Old Aberdeen in the years between the two world wars.

The manifestations in the house in College Bounds were described in a report by the Edinburgh Psychic College in 1949.

The minister's wife, Mrs Baird, giving her account to an Aberdeen advocate in 1938, said that from 1926 to 1927 onwards, the family had 'trouble' with the ghost in a back bedroom of the manse.

Two women guests who occupied the bedroom at different times were disturbed by a 'continuous sound of breathing in the room.'

Mrs Baird's sister-in-law had complained that she could not get a peaceful night's sleep because of the manifestations.

A Nurse Blair, who had been through the Great War, complained that the sound 'made her feel more nervous and more conscious of the next world than her experience during the time her hospital was being bombed in France.'

Nurse Blair reported that the breathing was not in itself alarming - 'it was just constant regular breathing as if someone had fallen asleep.'

The minister's small boy refused to sleep in the haunted room except with the light on, the door open and the company of a dog.

One night the dog was removed, the light switched off and the door shut. His mother told the psychic investigator:

'He wakened up screaming saying there was a clergyman sitting in the corner of the room sleeping over a book.'

After Nurse Blair left in the spring of 1937 Mrs Baird finally reported the haunting to the University principal.

According to the report by the Edinburgh Psychic College, he contacted a Glasgow minister, Rev William Reid, 'who evidently communicated with an unseen spirit who, he says, looks after him.

'The Rev Mr Reid asked his 'familiar' to find out in the spirit world what was happening that this small boy in Aberdeen could not sleep. His 'familiar' told him that he had been in communication with the spirit of Professor Johnstone (who formally occupied the manse) and asked him why he frightened that small boy.

'Professor Johnstone was very concerned and said, "It is not my intention to frighten anybody. I go back to the room I live in and read in and I sit down and I read a book and sometimes I fall asleep when I am reading.'

Soon after the haunting ceased.

On one occasion when the minister's son described the old clergyman a visitor said: 'Why, that's old Johnstone!'

As a child in Old Aberdeen, Katherine Trail visited a manse with a haunted reputation. The 'very quaint, large house' at the corner of the Chaplainry, was haunted by the ghost of a young child. The house was bought by a Mr Leslie who eventually knocked it down. During demolition workmen found bones built into a wall behind the fireplace. The bones were not human but the remains of a pheasant, a partridge and a rabbit!

I have personal knowledge of two former North-east manses with a supernatural history - one in Banff and Buchan and the other in the Kincardineshire Mearns.

A former colleague spent his childhood in the manse near Banff, and many years ago he gave me a vivid description of poltergeist activity experienced by the younger members of the family in a bedroom. Drawers were pulled from dressers by an unseen force, while his own bed rocked and tilted like a ship in a gale.

In the Fifties, while a district reporter with the *People's Journal*, I spent the afternoon in a manse which the occupant claimed was haunted.

As I sat on a sofa in the living room the lady assured me I would hear the sound of an object, resembling a heavy chest, being dragged across the floor of the bedroom directly above our heads. 'You can hear the noise most afternoons,' she said cheerfully.

Three children also lived in the house and they backed up this claim. I held my breath, but nothing unusual happened.

The lady of the house then took me on a tour of the old building, which stands in its own grounds near the sea.

She told of the day she walked into an unfurnished bedroom and was stunned to find that a four-poster bed had materialized in the corner behind the door. In the bed was a dying man. 'He was a very old man,' she told me, 'His breath rasped in his throat as he gasped for air, and his chest heaved with the effort.'

On another occasion a young lodger, his face pale with shock, told her a tall man in an old-fashioned frock coat had suddenly appeared beside him in the bathroom. This particular apparition had also been seen by the youngsters.

No ghosts showed up on that sunny afternoon 40 years ago. Years later I returned to the old manse and peeked through the iron gates. My hostess of yester-year had long left. An elderly gentleman was pruning roses but I did not have the heart to ask if his home was haunted!

The Church of Scotland hostel, Deeford, in Aberdeen's Riverside Drive, was frequently haunted by a ghost called Mary.

Mary was believed to be a minister's daughter, who gave birth to an illegitimate child. When the baby was taken from her poor Mary committed suicide in a bedroom on the second floor of the 19th century house.

For 20 years Mary's ghost made frequent visits to the granite villa overlooking the River Dee. She made her presence known by switching lights on and off, and sometimes witnesses heard the sound of breaking glass and the 'swishing' of her skirt. Apparently she was very active when young children were around. But after large-scale alterations were carried out at Deeford around 1973 - walls were knocked down and passages opened up - Mary's appearances became less and less.

Chapter Twenty

The Sobbing Child

A grey shroud of fog rolling in from the North Sea added to the atmosphere when I visited Stonehaven to hear about the strange case of the sobbing child.

It began one night in December 1992, as a young husband and wife relaxed at home. Upstairs their children were in bed. Then.....

The wife, her ears attuned to the least cry or whimper from the youngsters, rose quickly from her seat and dashed upstairs. It proved a false alarm. The children were safely tucked up in bed fast asleep.

But she did not tell her husband what had alarmed her. *It was the sobbing of a child!*

The truth emerged the very next day after her husband was confronted by a strange apparition on the same upper floor.

He told me of the eerie confrontation when I visited the detached turn-of-the-century dwelling house which stands on the edge of the seaside town.

That December morning he got up at around five-thirty. He left the bedroom and crossed the carpeted gallery which connects various rooms, including a bathroom.

As he reached for the light switch on a wall near the stairway he froze. His gaze fell on the bathroom which was about 30 feet from him. Although it was an early winter's morning, daylight filtered through the bathroom window.

He told me: 'The bathroom door was ajar and standing in the doorway was the figure of a young girl in an old-fashioned nightie.'

The girl was thin, with long dark hair and aged between five or six.

'She seemed real enough to me,' he went on. 'She was looking straight at me. I called out my daughter's name, but I knew it wasn't her.

'The child's left hand rested on the door knob. I never took my eyes off her as I switched on the light. She simply disappeared!'

He was not frightened by the experience. So far the couple have made no efforts to find out the history of the previous owners of the house.

Neither the wife nor their children have seen the strange girl. The couple have not mentioned the incident to them.

But his wife told me of other unusual occurrences which took place while she was alone in the house. Before moving in the couple did some refurbishment work. One day as the wife worked in the kitchen - she was rubbing down cupboards - she was suddenly overcome by a 'terrifying' feeling. She stopped what she was doing and fled the scene.

'I had a feeling that I was being watched,' she explained.

Another time she was upstairs when the cold water tap on a wash hand basin in a bedroom became activated. Water was gushing from the tap when she entered the room; 'I certainly didn't leave it running,' she said. 'I was pretty scared by that.'

The couple are level-headed and very responsible - the husband is a respected businessman - and they are not given to flights of superstitious fancy.

Despite the strange phenomena they say their home is a 'happy house, with a warm and friendly atmosphere.' I would not dispute that. However, the husband is not convinced it was a ghost he saw framed in the bathroom doorway, nor is he prepared to say the house is haunted.

Yet one other mystery lingers - the family dog refuses to cross the threshold of their daughter's bedroom! I suspect the animal can see or sense something which cannot be detected by its owners.

Chapter Twenty-one

The Ghost of Captain Beaton

Aberdeen's Old Militia Barracks, all turrets and crow-stepped gables, looks the sort of place to harbour a ghost.

Football fans might not give the building a second glance on the trek along King Street to Pittodrie Stadium, but ghost-hunters are intrigued by its paranormal history.

The former barracks, the depot of Grampian Transport, is haunted by a well-documented ghost, said to be the restless spirit of a Captain Beaton, an officer in the Gordon Highlanders.

Mention his name to a bus driver and you are sure to be greeted with a wide, knowing smile. 'Captain Beaton's Ghost' was first given prominence in the 1970s, after staff at the depot reported a series of strange occurrences.

Drivers avoided dining alone in the staff canteen while cleaners shunned a certain area of the depot.

John Law, a driver, was eating on his own in the canteen when he got a cold blast of air on the back of his neck, although there was no one else around. 'I could not see anyone,' he said. 'But when the same thing happened again I was down the stairs like a shot.'

There was also a report that a light switched on by itself.

Stories began to circulate of staff catching glimpses of a soldier in uniform. One man swore he saw a pair of feet with white spats, the sort worn in Highland regiments, ascending the stairs in front of him. Another saw a soldier in a greatcoat. Other times he was in the kilt.

The ghost is said to move eerily along the top floor and downstairs. He no longer haunts the canteen for it has been relocated.

The barracks date from 1861-63. In 1914 the military handed the building over to the old Aberdeen Corporation Tramways. Tramcars were garaged there, but following the outbreak of World War One the army moved back in again.

Why does the spirit of Captain Beaton stalk the building? The most popular theory is that he hanged himself before he was due to leave for France.

True or false? I contacted the Gordon Highlanders' Regimental Headquarters in Aberdeen to find out.

Well, a Captain Beaton *did* exist around the time of the First World War. But the spokesman was unable to throw any light on the mystery.

'Yes, there was a Captain Beaton, but where, how and when he died we are unable to say. We just don't know. We have nothing on record other than the fact a captain of that name was with the regiment at that time.'

There is no trace of a Captain Beaton dying during the campaign.

I scanned the columns of names of Gordons who died in the period 1914-19, while serving with regimental battalions or other units. They make tragic reading, but Captain Beaton is not listed. I found eight Beatons of whom the highest ranking was a Colour-Sergeant.

Military life abounds with tales of haunted barrack blocks.

A retired army officer with 50 years' service in Highland regiments told me of his early days at Fort George, the grim, wind-swept fortress built on the edge of the Moray Firth after the Forty-Five Uprising. 'The Fort' is supposed to be haunted by a phantom piper.

'There was always evidence of a piper playing, day or night, but whether it was a ghostly piper or someone else practising, who knows?' he said.

Fort George has fired the imagination of young soldiers to this day.

I have personal knowledge of the garrison 'ghost' while on sentry duty one snowy December night in 1954 - but it was the squeals of squabbling cats rather than the bagpipes that enlivened an otherwise dull and extremely lonely vigil.

In Moorish Castle Barracks in Gibraltar two years later clerks were reluctant to do night duty after 'mystery' footsteps were heard in the orderly room after 'lights out'. The old tale of an officer who hanged himself in a downstairs office, originally a guardroom, added to their anxiety. The footsteps were attributed to Orderly Officers.

I began to wonder if 'The Ghost of Captain Beaton' was the result of fertile imagination. But I am not so sure.

At the end of the First World War the barracks were handed back to Aberdeen Town Council. The tramcars started rolling again and because of a housing shortage the floors at the front of the barracks were used to house families.

Aberdeen-born Mrs May Cooper was a child when she lived in the officers' quarters in the barracks. Her family stayed there for 11 years, and her young sister was born there.

She told me: 'The front door of our flat was opposite a stair leading to a huge loft where clothes were dried in bad weather. The loft ran the entire length of the King Street frontage and was divided by brick walls. I was terrified to go up there because it was said there was a ghost. It was inclined to be dark and the washing made it very spooky.

'I vaguely remember being told that a soldier had hanged himself there but I don't know if this is true.'

If Mrs Cooper's memory serves her well that means the tale of the soldier who killed himself was common knowledge to families living in the former barracks in the 1920s.

I spoke to another Aberdeen lady who had knowledge of the ghost during the same period.

In fact, Mrs Helen Leiper, who is in her mid-seventies, saw the apparition while a child.

Mrs Leiper remembers the moment well, although it happened 70 years ago.

'We were visiting my mother's aunt who lived in the barracks,' she said. 'I got bored with grown-up gossip and wandered up-stairs.'

The young Helen stopped outside an open doorway. She looked inside a small room. Daylight streamed into the room. There was an iron cot with a white bed cover.

Sitting on the bed was a soldier. 'He was wearing a khaki uniform; he was not in the kilt,' Mrs Leiper told me. 'He had a bandage round his head and he appeared to be winding another bandage around his hands. I never saw his feet.'

The soldier did not look in the little girl's direction. Instead, he rose without a word and vanished into thin air. The bed was real enough.

Said Mrs Leiper: 'I hurried downstairs to tell the others what I had seen. But they did not believe me, putting it down to childish fantasy. But nothing they said would shake my belief.

'Many times after I related my experience to others. Then, about 15 years ago, I read for the first time that people working in the building had seen the ghost of a soldier. I immediately phoned my daughter in London, who was as thrilled as I was. At last I had silenced the sceptics!'

Chapter Twenty-two

Demons of the Hills

The fearful phantom of the high peaks - the Big Grey Man of Ben Macdhui - haunts the imagination of climbers and hillwalkers who set foot on Scotland's second highest mountain.

A glimpse of the grey giant, or the sound of his crunching footsteps, is enough to send the bravest rushing back down a mountain path.

The Ben Macdhui spectre, known in Gaelic as Am Fear Liath Mor, gained notoriety in 1925, when Professor John Norman Collie described how an unknown terror forced him to flee from the misty mountain 35 years earlier. He did not see the wraith but was frightened by the eerie 'crunch, crunch' of approaching footsteps. Professor Collic, who was an experienced climber, told the annual dinner of the Cairngorm Club, of which he was honorary president: 'Whatever you may make of it I do not know, but there is something very queer about the top of Ben Macdhui, and I will not go back there again by myself, I know.'

The legend of the Big Grey Man, which was not widespread in the last century, had echoes in the 'evil spirit' that prowled Creag-an-aibhse - the 'Rock of the Ghost' - near Braemar. The 'loathsome, black, shapeless, monstrous, huge' thing guarded the foot of the hill between sundown and sunrise. Amid fearful cries and dreadful noises it rolled down huge boulders and showers of stones on the unwary. A holy man erected a wooden cross on a cairn on the summit. He said prayers and banished the thing. In 1861 it was said that decayed splinters of the cross could still be found.

Over the years hillusers have encountered the Big Grey Man. While on leave in October 1943, Lance-Corporal Alexander 'Sandy' Tewnion heard strange, loud footsteps on the Coire Etchachan path. He turned and fired three shots at the 'strange shape' which charged out of the mist. Mr Tewnion, a retired schoolmaster, told me imagination and a thick mist were the cause.

Experienced mountaineers blame weather conditions on the strange phenomena - the ghostly sounds, the gigantic figures and the weird, haunting music. Aberdeen author Robert Smith tells of the time he watched a huge figure approach him out of the mist on Ben Macdhui, only to be greeted by a friendly tourist. The 'Brocken Spectre', a trick of light and mist, is not only encountered in the Harz Mountains.

But there have been far weirder sightings of mountain spectres in the Cairngorms.

The late Dr George Duncan, Aberdeen advocate, Hon. Sheriff-Substitute of Aberdeen, and Chairman of the Aberdeen Education Committee, wrote to *The Scotsman* on 21 October 1941. He told of a bizarre experience after he had come off Cairntoul and the aptly named Devil's Point at dusk one September around the year 1914.

His climbing companion was James A. Parker, mountaineer, photographer and future president of the Cairngorm Club. They were being driven in a dog-cart to Braemar from Derry Lodge, with Duncan in the back seat, looking backwards at the passing scenery.

'All at once,' said Duncan, 'halfway to the Linn of Dee, I got the shock of my life, by seeing before me a tall figure in a black robe - the conventional figure of the Devil himself - clad in long depending sleeves and waving his arms towards me. I got such a shock that I felt what I never felt before or since, a cold shiver running down my spine. In a minute or two the dog-cart turned a corner and the figure passed from view. Afterwards, my friend asked why I had suddenly become silent (we were in the middle of a conversation), and I told him then what I had seen. I have often visited the spot since in the endeavour to locate trees the waving branches of which might have explained the appearance, but without any satisfactory result.'

Mr Parker substantiated the strange story in the *Cairngorm Club Journal* in July 1916: 'What it was that Duncan actually saw we cannot tell now, although we have both driven over the same road since then, and kept our eyes glued to the hillside in hope of seeing His Majesty, but failed to see anything that could even suggest him. Yet Duncan must have seen something, as he was so scared that he did not speak for half an hour afterwards, and had not the presence of mind to stop the trap so that the driver and I might see the gentleman for ourselves.'

But consider another chilling apparition Tom Crowley met in the spring of 1922 or 1923.

Crowley, a former president of a mountaineering club in Moray, spoke 'very freely and earnestly' about the experience to associates.

It happened when he was descending from Braeriach, the third highest mountain in the UK, and the source of the River Dee. He was making for the tower bothy in Glen Einich: 'when he heard footsteps behind him. He looked over his shoulder and saw a huge grey misty figure.'

'He stopped and faced it, and declared that he made out, in the otherwise inarticulated misty figure, a shape like a head 'with two peaked ears', and also legs with talons more like fingers than toes. He was terror-stricken and ran.'

Who can blame him?

Chapter Twenty-three

The De'il at Baldarroch

S heep, deer and goats are the only cloven-hoofed beasts you'll find amid the rolling countryside around Crathes.

But in 1838 superstitious country folk firmly believed Auld Hornie himself was up to his devilish tricks at Baldarroch Farm.

They came from miles around to gape at the small granite farmhouse, which stands near a busy road junction of the North Deeside Road at Crathes. They composed jaunty ballads about 'The De'il o' Baldarroch'. Johnny Milne o' Leevit's Glen - Glenlivet - smuggler turned poet - and fellow chapmen hawked versions of the 'clodding' throughout North-east Scotland.

A verse from Alexander Walker's poem sets the scene:

The spoons an' dishes, knives and forks,
They frisked aboot as light as corks,
An' cups an' ladles joined the dancing,
An' thro' the house they a' gaed prancing.

Invisible forces terrified the occupants at Baldarroch. Farm implements were moved around at will; cooking utensils were disarranged and found in out of the way places on the farm; stones, peats, potatoes and other missiles rained down on unsuspecting heads. Gossips added to the legend. Did peats in the stack flit from place to place? Was the washing pitched up onto the roof of the house? What unseen hand cleaned the 'greeps' in the stables? But the line was drawn when it was whispered the milk churn rolled out to meet the farmer and danced a jig round him 'like a Newfoundland dog!'

The 'clodding' continued for weeks until the 7th Baronet of Leys, Sir Thomas Burnett, ordered an investigation into the mysterious goings-on.

Two investigators, a writer and a kirk elder, arrived at Baldarroch to find a group of persons 'with long faces' in the farm kitchen.

James Thomson, a mason, assured the visitors that the strange occurrences at the farm were authentic. 'When I was sitting here last night,' he said, 'I saw the spurtle come through the stone (he pointed to the chimney brace) and fly butt (through) the house.' While taking a pinch of snuff a stone dropped through the floor above and struck his snuff box, snapping the lid shut and bruising his fingers.

Earlier Thomson told the incredulous investigators: 'I was sitting upstairs in the garret last afternoon when I observed an old shoe running in the crap o' the wa', when I laid hold of it, but was unable to stop it.'

The 'ghostbusters' suspected a young servant girl, 'who looked like one enjoying the fun.' But they left the house in a hurry when a careless remark annoyed the assembled group.

The parish minister and the baronet's brother then visited Baldarroch. They found the servant girl washing potatoes in a tub of water in the kitchen, and saw how by some slight of hand she made the tatties squirt through her fingers and across the floor. She cried they would not stay in the tub.

A report was sent to the Procurator Fiscal in Stonehaven. The servant girl and another young lass suspected of aiding her in the cantrips, together with witnesses, gave evidence. Whatever the outcome of the inquiry the 'clodding' stopped.

It was later claimed the whole affair had been an elaborate plot against the farmer. He had resigned the tenancy to a younger son, to the fury of the elder son and certain members of the family. The 'clodding' was devised as a way of playing on his superstitions and force him to change his decision.

After moving to Baldarroch in August 1991 tenants Stewart and Carol McGuire told me about some inexplicable happenings. Carol saw the figure of an old woman in the front garden. The woman was tall and thin with grey hair tied back. Carol had no feeling of dread when she saw the apparition.

However, Carol reported a 'cold, creepy' atmosphere in the byre and some outbuildings, resulting in a sudden drop in temperature. This did not occur when animals were present. On one occasion when she was gripped by an unknown terror while working alone in the byre Carol sang the opening lines of the hymn, *Onward Christian Soldiers*.

Her husband Stewart, who is a farrier, confirmed a similar drop in temperature in the byre when the horses were grazing in the fields. As he was doing a welding job in the byre one night a noise like 'a galloping horse' shook the rafters.

If the De'il has left his mark at Baldarroch, the McGuires refuse to bat an eyelid. It is not the first time they have lived in a house with a haunted reputation. For seven years they stayed in a former mill in Lanarkshire, where the ghost of an old man made unscheduled appearances.

So much for the 'De'il o' Baldarroch'. But in more recent times Crathes had an even stranger 'haunting'. It was more 'poultrygeist' than poltergeist!

I refer to Muriel, the red leghorn hen, who almost rivalled the Feathered Phantom of Lincoln's Inn a ghostly creature that left footprints on a powdered floor during a psychic investigation in London in 1901.

Muriel was a family pet for many years until she died in 1993. Jenny Watson, a local councillor, told me how Muriel regularly sat in the kitchen and sipped coffee and was hand-fed.

Two days after her husband, Dr Adam Watson, buried the hen she distinctly heard a scraping noise below her table.

Jenny wasn't in the least bit frightened. She knew it was Muriel! She shouted on the hen to stop, and the scraping noises ceased. The same thing happened the following day. Friends suggested it was the family dog, but Jenny said it was definitely the sound of Muriel's claws she had heard.

So there was absolutely no question of summoning an 'eggs-orcist!'

Chapter Twenty-four

A Strange and Seeing Time

'I turned to the right - in total horror.'
American novelist Elizabeth Byrd was alone in bed when she came face to face with the ghost of Leith Hall.

Between the dressing table and the foot of the four-poster bed in the second floor master bedroom stood a man.

Elizabeth described him thus: 'He was as solid as any man so that he didn't seem in the least like an apparition. I saw him for perhaps two minutes. Since I was still lying with my head on the pillow he may have appeared taller than he actually was - but he seemed about six foot, and massively built but not fat. His head was bandaged in dirty white so that I couldn't see his eyes, but I felt that they were looking straight into mine. He had a dark beard. I can't state what sort of shirt he wore but he stood with his legs wide apart in tight, dark green trousers. Both arms were apart, too - a very challenging stance. I can't swear to this but I think his left hand held a short, thick weapon, not a knife but wider than a sword.'

Terrified, Elizabeth screamed: 'Go away! Go away!' The figure disappeared in the direction of the window behind the dressing table, and Elizabeth fled downstairs, never again to sleep in that room.

In the spring of 1966, Elizabeth, author of the best seller, *Immortal Queen*, the story of Mary Queen of Scots, rented a wing of the drum-towered, white-faced mansion near Kennethmont in Aberdeenshire.

Leith Hall fired her creative powers and she wrote of her two-year stay in *A Strange and Seeing Time*, sub-titled, *Life in a Haunted Castle* (Hale, 1971).

Soft footfalls, sometimes a slow shuffling, other times a patter such as a child or a puppy might make, were discounted by her as sheer imagination. But a door slamming on a windless summer night made her think twice.

Elizabeth went in search of the identity of the bedroom phantom. The Leiths of Leith Hall built their house in 1650 and stayed there for almost 300 years. They were staunch Jacobites and the family had strong military connections, with Leiths fighting in the Peninsula Wars, the Crimea (Colonel Alexander Sebastian Leith-Hay was one of the 'Thin-Red-Line' at Balaclava), and in the Indian Mutiny (where Sebastian acquired a Hindustani-speaking cockatoo called Cocky).

She discounted Sebastian. Although he had a beard he was never wounded during his campaigns.

Instead she plumped for John Leith of Leith Hall, who was shot in a drunken quarrel in Aberdeen a few nights before Christmas 1763. The laird was carousing with cronies in Archie Campbell's tavern in the Castlegate when events turned ugly and an argument sprang up between Leith and Abernethy of Mayen.

As the tavern emptied a shot rang out - and Leith collapsed on the Plainstones outside. A pistol ball was lodged in his brain. He was carried to a nearby house where he died on Christmas Day, his faithful wife and eldest son at his bedside. Abernethy fled the country. He claimed they had fought a duel and that he himself had been wounded. But murder was suspected and Harriot, who was expecting her fourth child, swore vengeance. Abernethy was outlawed and his family ruined.

Elizabeth Byrd was intrigued by a poem which appeared in the book, *Trustie to the End*, by the Hon. Mrs Henrietta Leith-Hay, mother of the 23rd and last laird of Leith Hall. (Mrs Leith-Hay, now deceased, who gave the house and estate to The National Trust for Scotland in 1945, never believed her home was haunted, although her husband, Charles Leith-Hay, had the gift of 'spirit writing').

The poem told how:
Leith's servant bound the bleeding head
And bore him to his bed

So the bandaged phantom that menaced Elizabeth in the master bedroom on 16 July 1968 might have been poor John Leith. Elizabeth said she had seen no portrait which could identify the ghost, but one exists in Leith Hall. And the 'luckless laird' is beardless! Ironically, he is posing with a firearm and powder flask. The mystery of Elizabeth's phantom deepens!

Elizabeth experienced other unexplained happenings at Leith Hall - phantom bagpipe music with counterpoint of drums, a chanted Mass, and the ghostly smells of camphor and food in her bedroom.

Guests also reported supernatural phenomena.

Novelist Alanna Knight, her husband Alistair and their two young sons, stayed at Leith Hall in the autumn of 1968. On a previous visit Alanna had an extraordinary series of 'waking dreams', which whisked her back to a Victorian nursery.

But when she and Alistair spent the night in the haunted bedroom - their boys slept in another room - they experienced an uncanny sensation.

When she spoke to me about that October night, Alanna said: 'We both woke up feeling there was somebody else in the room. I had a feeling of being smothered. It was a terrifying experience.'

Alistair recalled: 'I had a feeling of discomfort, as if someone was pressing their face close to mine. The room was black as treacle.'

In the early hours of the morning Alanna was wakened by the sound of a woman's laughter. This was followed by the 'tinkle of crystal, rustle of taffeta or stiff silk, and subdued talk', as if a party was going on around her in the darkened bedroom. Her husband heard nothing.

Alanna has since returned to the mansion - and still finds it 'a very creepy place'. Her husband agreed that when they first went to the house in the Sixties it had a 'real eerie feeling', but the fact that a wing had been unheated did not help. Since full heating was installed the 'eeriness' had lifted.

Heavy snow fell during Elizabeth Byrd's last Hogmanay at Leith Hall. The guests included Alanna and Alistair Knight and Alanna's mother, who was in complete ignorance of the ghosts. But during the night Alanna's mother awoke to the sound of two loud bangs, like pistol shots. Heavy footsteps 'like a military man in nailed boots' rang out. The noises were never explained.

The previous year writer Iain Parr was invited to spend the week-end at Leith Hall. On the first night, as he lay awake in bed in a darkened, top floor bedroom, he was suddenly pulled up to a sitting position.

Parr wrote of his experience in the *Weekly Scotsman* in April 1967: 'It was quite involuntary on my part. Whatever it was I was allowed to flop back. I switched on the light and examined my pyjama jacket. It was not disarrayed but I assure you something had pulled me from the pillow.'

Elizabeth Byrd was to recall many times her 'strange and seeing time' at Leith Hall, and the effect the period had on her life. She would never forget the mansion, a place of romance - (there is a

365-day clock which, by family tradition, is rewound on August 12) - and of mystery. It is approached by a long tree-lined drive where the infamous 'dool' tree grows; a sycamore from which felons were hanged.

Sadly, Elizabeth died in her native United States in 1989.

She was a good friend of Scotland. After Leith Hall, Elizabeth moved to the Mill of Inver in Royal Deeside. Her love of the country and its people is reflected in her warm and human touch.

Her last request was that her ashes be scattered on Arthur's Seat, the noble hill overlooking Edinburgh.

And what of the ghosts of Leith Hall?

When I visited Leith Hall in the summer of 1994 I was firmly put in my place when I asked two young lady guides if it was haunted.

I suggested they read Elizabeth Byrd's book. I didn't have the heart to tell them that this most charming of North-east houses was once the subject of a BBC television documentary on ghosts which was broadcast on Hallowe'en!

Chapter Twenty-five

Footsteps from Beyond

'The night we saw our ghost will never leave my memory,' wrote Fiona Campbell. I cannot blame her.

Fiona and her husband James were spending a summer weekend at a farm cottage near the small town of Kintore in rural Aberdeenshire. The year was 1980.

They were the guests of Fiona's mother and step-father, and had often travelled to the parish of Kinellar from their home in Caithness.

The cottage sat at the end of a narrow road, surrounded by fields. In front of the house stretched a field of turnips, while in a field at the back cattle grazed on higher ground, up a steep bank.

The cottage had been modernised and had a sun porch at the front.

Fiona and James's bedroom was also at the front of the house. They had a splendid view of the countryside from their bed. Her step-father's collie dog, Jura, had given birth to a litter of pups and, as it was more a pet than a working dog, it slept in the kitchen, next to the couple's bedroom.

In the early hours of a fine, clear morning the young couple were wakened by Jura's whimpering. 'Normally,' said Fiona, 'if she heard anyone around the house Jura would bark. But this time she was whimpering and moving around restlessly.

'Then we heard a 'dragging' sound - and heavy footsteps - coming from the back of the house. Then we saw it. A black shape of a man, through the window, bent double and walking backwards as if he was dragging something heavy.'

Slowly, the figure moved past their vantage point. It stooped over its load, went back a couple of steps, then began to drag the unseen load along the ground.

Fiona and James talked in whispers. They couldn't believe what happened next. *Instead of moving around the sun-porch the figure walked straight through it as if it had never been built!*

'I cannot begin to describe our fear,' said Fiona. 'It wasn't like anything we had ever experienced before. Shortly after, the noise faded and the dog settled down.'

The couple sought an explanation from their hosts the next morning. It was suggested a farm worker had been removing a dead beast from a field.

Fiona told me: 'There was no way anyone could get a beast over the fence and down the steep bank. They would have had to drag it through an access gate. Anyway, no beasts died that night and none of the men had been out.

'We are convinced we saw a ghost. Never before or since have either of us felt the same cold fear.'

John and Moyra Argo's home stands on the brow of the Spital, an ancient highway with one foot in Old Aberdeen. It faces east and on the day I called a breeze ruffled the white-capped North Sea, so close you felt you could touch it.

The title deeds of their house stretch back to August 1746 - four months after Culloden. In the 12th century a hospital, or Spital, for infirm priests, and a chapel, stood in what is now St Peter's Cemetery. No great distance away, on the east side of King's Crescent, the ruins of the Lepers' House could still be seen in the middle of the 17th century.

History and hauntings are in the air.

In 1966, a year after the Argo family moved into the two-storey house, strange things began to happen. In those days New Pitsligo-born John was a self-employed baker. His bakehouse stood in the back garden while the shop was situated on the ground floor.

One winter evening John and Moyra were relaxing in their living room when a sound like heavy footsteps was heard on the stairway leading from the upstairs bedrooms. The footsteps stopped at the door of the front living room. John threw open the door. The hallway was deserted. 'I ran upstairs to check on our young children (three sons and a daughter) but they were fast asleep in their beds,' John told me.

The mysterious thumps and banging continued. They were also heard in the bakehouse, where John worked all hours. They did not worry the Argos but John's part-time assistant refused to work alone at night in the bakehouse.

On another occasion the couple had a woman visitor when their amiable conversation was halted by three loud knocks on the front door. John got to the door in moments but there was no one outside. Said Moyra: 'Our friend went pure white and said "There's going to be a death!" Thankfully, she was wrong.'

112

John claimed his mother and sister were psychic, and recalled two instances when odd happenings - a picture toppling from a wall and a clock stopping - heralded sudden deaths.

Even the family dog, Kim, a black labrador, saw 'something'. For several minutes it stared at a spot on the living room wall and no amount of coaxing by its owners detracted the animal from its uncanny gaze.

But the most curious incident occurred while the Argos slept in a bed settee in the same room.

John awoke unexpectedly to find *a tramp with a dog crossing the floor.*

The man was short and fat, hatless, and wore a gaberdine-style coat, tied around the waist with a piece of twine. The man's face was turned away from John, so he did not recognise the intruder. The tramp was leading a black and white dog on the end of a string. John told me: 'He was a solid-looking figure but when he reached the centre of the room he simply vanished. I first saw him as he appeared from the wall cupboard which was shut at the time, I did not alert my wife but waited until the next morning before I told her what I had seen.'

The unexplained noises carried on for many years but stopped when the bakehouse was demolished and refurbishment work was carried out on a neighbouring property.

Was there some undetected psychic cause? To this day the Argos remain baffled.

Did the house have a haunted reputation before they moved in? The only clue might be the fact that before the last war a previous owner died under tragic circumstances.

I was informed of two other 'haunted' houses in the vicinity.

A former neighbour told the Argos she had frequently seen a lady in Victorian dress in her Spital home.

In Froghall Terrace, just round the corner, an old house was said to be haunted in the summer of 1958 by a 'hair-raising figure in a white shroud.'

Neighbours scoffed at claims that the 200-year-old cottage was haunted, but it was no laughing matter for an elderly widow and her 20-year-old daughter in whose home the apparition first appeared.

They were wakened in their upstairs bedroom to find the ghost approaching slowly from the direction of the tiny window. They screamed - and the thing vanished. After the incident they refused to sleep in the room.

The next person to see the thing was a young woman guest who was sleeping downstairs. She woke up while it was still dark and saw the apparition standing beside the piano. The terrified woman screamed, fled from the room and jumped into the bed occupied by the mother and daughter.

Interviewed by a newspaper reporter, the widow believed the apparition was an omen. Her upstairs bedroom window overlooked a cottage where her brother-in-law was born. When the ghost first appeared he was seriously ill. He died soon after.

Twenty-years ago an ex-merchant navyman, Robert Cowe, greeted a ghostly visitor in his bedroom at his former home in High Street, Fraserburgh.

He read in bed until midnight and was contemplating rising to get a cigarette. The room was in darkness and all was quiet in the old, three-storey building, which he later described as 'eerie.'

Mr Cowe looked over the edge of his bed and saw a pair of well-pointed black shoes with buckles. His startled gaze moved upwards. He took in black stockings, a blue and white checked dress - and then the face of an old woman with ginger hair, who was stooping over his bed. She wore a pleading expression, as if seeking help.

Mr Cowe twice asked the ghost: 'What do you want?', but the figure disappeared. He found the experience 'shattering.'

(You don't have to live in an old house to host a ghost - I know someone who reported ghostly happenings in a high-rise flat off Aberdeen's Union Street.)

Number 27 Blackfriars Street in Aberdeen had a history of phantom footsteps until the empty and barred dwelling house was demolished to make way for the Denburn link road.

'Strange things were happening there all the time,' Mrs Kath Innes told me.

Kath and her mother occupied attic rooms during World War One while her father served with the Gordon Highlanders on the Western Front.

Kath's mother only learned of the house's haunted reputation after they had moved in, and they stayed less than a year. There was the occasion a neighbour was roused by the patter of bare feet across the floor of her kitchen. The sound stopped at the fireplace, but, on investigating, she found her family fast asleep. The next morning the woman was informed her son had been killed in France. (I later received corroboration of this uncanny incident).

Another time Kath's mother was scolding her after a domestic accident when there was a thunderous knock at the door. Said Kath: 'We both got a shock and when my mother opened the door there was nobody there! The house had a bare wooden stair yet not a footstep was heard going up or down.'

Kath also recalled the occasion she and her mother were chatting to an elderly woman neighbour at her door when there was a terrific crash from inside. On checking the neighbour found that a huge family bible had inexplicably landed flat on the floor from the top of a chest of drawers in her bedroom.

The mystery sounds intrigued Kath. Perhaps they had something to do with the fact the house was built in the former grounds of a 13th century Dominican monastery? A Black Friar's sandal was found yards away during construction of Aberdeen Art Gallery in the 1880s.

So-called 'crisis apparitions' were common during the war years when loved ones at home saw their menfolk at the exact time they died. During my research for this book I was told of another uncanny incident involving a Gordon Highlander during World War One. My informant was related to the persons involved.

America was at war, and the Russian Czar had abdicated. On the Western Front there was a glimmer of hope as British troops advanced to a depth of three miles and captured 11,000 German prisoners.

It was April 1917, and the sounds of war seemed a long way off as a signalman worked through the night at Portlethen railway station, on the main coastal line, a few miles south of Aberdeen.

In the early hours of the morning a bell in the signal box alerted him that a train had entered his section of the line.

The train passed and he turned to make a cup of tea.

Standing in the doorway of the signal box was a young soldier in the uniform of the Gordon Highlanders. The signalman was surprised to see his younger brother. After all, only a few days before he had returned to France after spending a leave at home.

'My God, what are you doing here?', he asked.

The soldier said he had called in past to say hello.

Just then the bell rang again. The train was leaving the stretch of line. When the railwayman turned to resume their conversation his brother had vanished! There was no sign of him anywhere.

The signalman's mind was in a turmoil and he could barely wait to finish his shift at six in the morning.

He raced home to tell his wife about the strange encounter. Before he opened his mouth she exclaimed: 'Heavens, you are as white as a ghost!'

He could not sleep nor eat his food for thinking of the meeting with his brother. Instead he went to see his mother in Newtonhill, and arrived as a telegram boy turned away from the front door.

His brother had died of wounds in a French hospital - on his 21st birthday!

Chapter Twenty-six

The Magic Cottage

The Glens of Foudland is a wild, hilly and desolate spot, even though the A96 hums with traffic winding through a stretch of countryside that is part of the vocabulary of weather forecasters and AA patrols in winter months.

This is a true story of what happened to a young couple who rented a cottage, a former farm cottar house, in the glens during the winter of 1991-92

The couple are married and hold down professional jobs. What they experienced on two nights during the nine months they stayed in the house was enough to test their stoical disbelief in the supernatural.

The owner of the cottage in question was living abroad when the couple moved in. They were on a short-term lease as their future home was under construction elsewhere in Aberdeenshire.

The cottage was built in the last century, perhaps earlier, but it was modernised to a high standard. Only the old barn, a haven for pigeons and other winged creatures of the night, was in need of urgent repairs.

The lady of the house admitted it was not love at first sight when she first saw the cottage. 'It would not have been out of place in *Wuthering Heights*,' she told me. 'It was really creepy at night.'

The first strange incident occurred in January 1992 when the couple returned late one Sunday night from Glasgow, a city they like to visit.

Before leaving on their week-end shopping jaunt they had set the living room fire for their return. Kindling and paper, but no paraffin.

They were cold and tired after the journey but decided to have something to eat before bed. They saw no point in lighting the fire. They heated some canned soup in the micro-wave, and settled down on the sofa with steaming bowls of broth to watch Joan Bakewell on TV.

It was at that point the fire lit itself!

The husband told me: 'I have not told too many people, a close friend or two, for fear of ridicule. But I swear the fire burst into flames without a match. And remember there could have not been any residual heat - the grate was cold when we left for Glasgow on the Friday. We were absolutely amazed, but it really did not hit us until the following morning.'

The second inexplicable happening took place a few nights later.

A storm lashed the darkened house when the husband drove home from work in Aberdeen. The belt of trees surrounding the cottage bent in the high wind, and icy fingers of rain tapped at the car windows. His heart missed a beat when the headlights picked out the front door, wide open to the night.

He recalled: 'I thought we had been burgled - and for all I knew they were still inside. I kept the car engine running just in case, and moved warily inside the house.'

He switched on the lights. He was alone and their home was untouched.

Except......

Since moving into their home he had been unable to coax an old clock back to life. It came with the tenancy. The chiming clock sat on the stone mantelpiece in the living room.

Yet when he entered the room the clock was merrily ticking - *and the hands were set at the correct time!*

'I can tell you that the front door played up from time to time,' he added. 'It was inclined to stick, and I cannot be certain if I had closed it properly when leaving for work earlier that day. It might have been blown open by the wind. But I cannot explain away the clock. I got home before my wife. We didn't touch it. The winding key was still under the clock when I arrived.'

The couple did not see or hear any ghosts during their stay. Nor did they know the history of the cottage.

But several times the wife experienced a sudden sharp fall in temperature in the living room, even with a roaring fire. 'It got so cold you could see the vapour from your breath,' she told me.

She began to dread spending the evening alone in the house. On the nights her husband was working late she waited for him in the car, the radio keeping her mind off whatever waited in the cottage.

Was their first home haunted?

Said the husband philosophically: 'I didn't believe in ghosts - and I still don't believe in ghosts. But I have no explanations for these incidents.'

118

Said his wife: 'I believe there are things for which we can't find logical explanations. I think there was something in that house, but I can't explain what.'

Whatever walks the old cottar house in the Glens of Foudland no longer walks alone. The house is once again occupied.

Chapter Twenty-Seven

Out of the Blue

The North Sea is a raging beast in a storm and through the centuries it has become the graveyard of many fine ships and their crews.

In the summer of 1990 a ghostly incident took place on Chevron's Ninian Southern oil production platform, 90 miles north-east of Shetland, which may have its roots in a shipwreck that happened *seventy years earlier!*

The mystery began when Glaswegian Bill McCluskey, a contract painter, turned in after a day's blasting and spraying work.

Bill was allotted a two-man cabin in the new living quarters after a previous occupier, a Geordie, had changed rooms. Bill thought nothing of the man's decision at the time.

Bill, who is in his fifties, slept in a bottom bunk with his feet pointing towards the door of the cabin. He had his bunk curtains wide open so he had a clear view of the cabin door. His companion in the bunk above chose to sleep with his curtains shut so heard or saw nothing.

During the night Bill woke up suddenly to find two strangers in the cabin. *A man and woman dressed in sailing gear from the 1920s!*

'I wasn't dreaming - they were standing almost at the cabin door,' he told me.

'The couple were standing close together and they were talking, although I could not hear a sound. They looked as if they were worried by something. They were holding hands too - the woman was holding her companion's left hand and he was holding her right hand.'

Bill described the couple as tall, although the man was taller. The man had grey hair and was wearing grey flannels, woollen pullover and white shoes. The woman was dressed in grey-striped jacket, blouse, short-sleeved jacket like a waistcoat and white shoes. She reminded Bill of 'Mrs Simpson - the late Duchess of Windsor'. Her hair was greyish and was brushed back over her ears. They were bare-headed and were not wearing life-jackets. They looked as if they were dressed for a yacht.

120

The room was in darkness - it had no porthole - and the electric lighting had been switched off. But Bill was able to distinguish the two figures, thanks to a light shining in their faces.

'The figures were solid-looking,' Bill added. 'When I first saw them I thought it was real people who had wandered into the cabin. I made no attempt to speak to them and as far as I know they did not seem to notice I was there.'

Bill sat up in bed and coolly lit a cigarette but extinguished it after two puffs.

He watched the man and woman for a minute before they vanished into thin air.

'It didn't bother me - I fell asleep soon after,' said Bill. 'I didn't tell any of the lads the next day - they would just have laughed.'

Bill believes the apparitions were of two people who perished in a yachting accident in the Twenties.

After leaving Ninian Southern - he was contracted for six weeks - Bill told his wife Ellen.

No one else knew of the weird encounter offshore until a second unexplained incident occurred in the vicinity of the Ninian Field two years later.

On the night of 26 September 1992, Shetland Coastguards initiated an investigation into the broadcasting of a Mayday call, which sounded 'like an electronic voice'. Standby safety vessels, which keep a round-the-clock watch on installations in the oilfield, launched an immediate search of the area, but nothing was found.

After the story was publicised Bill McCluskey broke his silence, and spoke of his ghostly encounter on Ninian Southern two years before. He believed that the mystery SOS voice was a ghostly distress call from the past.

Bill's strange story was reported by the oil company's in-house publication, *Chevron Times,* which described how: 'Ninian Central Platform Radio Operator Dave Moxey heard a Mayday call on distress channel 16 which he described as "digitised", like an electronic voice heard on telephones from talking computers.

'The single word "Mayday" was repeated seven or eight times. Shetland Coastguard, the Brent platform and ships in the area heard it too', he said. "We put out a message every half an hour asking for the caller to identify themselves but there was no response."'

The *Chevron Times* quoted Shetland author and journalist Jim

Nicolson who was consulted on whether there could be any supernatural connection. Jim said he was 'keeping an open mind' about the source of the voices, but explained many ships had sunk around the islands and wrecks were known to have been washed in the direction of the Ninian Field.

In the last century many herring drifters were lost in fearful storms and on one night alone, 58 men were drowned when 16 boats foundered.

Whether it was a ghostly call or a stupid hoax that was picked up has never been resolved.

However, a senior coastguard officer told me that the 'synthesized voice' was thought to have been broadcast by mistake by a piece of recording equipment offshore. It was not malicious - rather a false alarm.

But Bill McCluskey, who is now an employee of Nairn District Council, is still not convinced. 'I still think it could have been a voice from the past.'

Something else troubles him. Why did the Geordie who shared a cabin on Ninian Southern with his mate vacate his bunk and go elsewhere? Had he shared an eerie experience on a previous stay?

'It makes you think,' commented Bill.

Chapter Twenty-eight

The Lair of the White Lady

The omens looked good (depending on your point of view) when I set out for the lair of the White Lady of Edzell Castle. A seemingly impenetrable grey mist blanketed the Cairn-a-Mounth and it was not hard to imagine a time when travellers on the old drove road were menaced by robbers lurking in Thieves' Bush, a ravine near the summit.

Just across the Kincardineshire border the red-stoned ruins of the castle rise in a lofty mass a mile west of the Angus village that shares its name.

The castle, which overlooks a magnificent walled garden, or pleasance, was the home of one family - the 'lichtsome Lindsays' - from the late 15th century to the middle of the 18th century, when the last earl died, and the buildings were despoiled.

The White Lady is believed to be the ghost of Catherine Campbell, the second wife of David Lindsay, the ninth earl. History tells how Catherine, the richest widow in Scotland, was pronounced dead at Brechin Castle in October 1578. Legend has it she was epileptic and had fallen into a coma.

Her body was wrapped in a shroud and draped in jewels before being conveyed to the family vault in Edzell Cemetery, near the castle. The death watch was overseen by a sexton on the nights before the Lady of Edzell was entombed. On the eve of the burial greed overcame grief, and, by a guttering candle the sexton attempted to steal the precious gems. The good lady gave a sigh and awoke from her coma. She promised the sexton he could keep her jewels if he conducted her back to the castle. The guilty man fled into the night. Somehow Catherine dragged herself back to her home and pleaded with a terrified guard to open the gates. He refused and the following morning she was found dead from exposure. The sexton was hanged.

The melancholy mystery of the White Lady became newspaper headlines in March 1994 after American Carole Rollman took some black and white photographs of the great square tower from the south-east corner of the garden.

When she developed the photos it looked as if the ghostly image of a woman was gazing from a window on the second floor.

Carole thought: 'Wow! I caught a ghost.'

The weekly newspaper, *Montrose Review*, ran Carole's photograph and a full story with the front page headline, 'GOTCHA GHOST!' In interviews castle curator Geoff Hutson and gardener David Jamieson both admitted they were baffled by the picture.

After all, the window at the centre of the mystery is about 15 feet above the modern timber floor installed for visitors by Historic Scotland, the castle trustees.

Carole later checked out the location and when I talked to her she was no longer convinced she had photographed something supernatural. The 'ghost' was probably a combination of light and markings on the fabric wall. 'It seems the camera does lie,' added Carole.

But the story does not end there.

The enterprising *Review* enlisted the help of a professional psychic and clairvoyant to solve the mystery. Wendy Stanford-Taylor had never before visited Edzell Castle. She was not told of Carole Rollman's photograph nor of the 'White Lady' haunting.

Wendy told the paper that a 'powerful, melancholy spirit' was roaming the castle and garden. She added: 'As soon as I opened the garden gate I felt giddy. A heavy presence weighed down on me and all around me, but there was nothing to be frightened of. It wasn't evil. There was just a tremendous feeling of sadness.'

The roof and windows of the great tower house were open to a grey, leaden sky as I negotiated the narrow, twisting stairways of the castle, which once entertained Mary Queen of Scots. Swallows, swifts and house martins flitted through the spacious great hall.

On my arrival I was told of the existence of a photograph by a Montrose woman which purports to show a ghostly face.

Dogs 'sense' a supernatural presence - and at Edzell I learned of instances where dogs belonging to visitors simply refused to enter certain parts of the castle - particularly a kitchen area. One witness told me how a dog sat at the threshold of a room 'with its hackles up.'

The trim boxwood hedges in the garden spell out the Lindsay family motto: *Dum Spiro Spero* (While I Breathe I Hope).

It proved appropriate for I was rewarded with an interview with a man who was confronted by a weird apparition in the garden early one morning in February 1987.

David Jamieson, who is in his early sixties, unlocked the door connecting the turreted summer house with the castle garden, which he tends with loving care.

'I was frozen with fear,' he said. 'A few paces in front of me was something resembling a piece of white lace. When I stepped forward it moved back. When I stopped it stopped. It was a little taller than me and gave off a horrible, sickly smell, like strong pipe tobacco. After a few seconds it vanished.' Was it the White Lady?

David, a powerfully-built man from the Moray Firth area, gave a slight shudder at the memory. 'Exactly what it was I don't know. I was very frightened - but it was not evil.'

David mentioned his experience to psychic Wendy Stanford-Taylor and she suggested the smell he detected might have been due to embalming fluid.

At certain times of the year fog clings to the landscape, but David denied the 'thing' was a wisp of fog.

He told me that a motorist was driving past the cemetery (where the Lindsay vault is located) at night when he saw 'something resembling a plastic sheet' in his headlights. The driver didn't stop to investigate.

David Jamieson and Geoff Hutson both experienced a strange occurrence at precisely the same moment. The gardener and the curator were in different parts of the tower house when they thought they were on the point of bumping into someone on the stairs. But there was nobody there.

Geoff Hutson, castle curator for 15 years, has spotted the White Lady on three separate occasions. He was on leave when I arrived on my ghost quest, but when I eventually caught up with him the Oxfordshire man described the sightings.

He twice saw the White Lady in 1986. Their paths crossed for the first time in the castle garden. No one had visited the castle that particular day and he was surprised when he saw a figure walking along a footpath. A few weeks later the apparition appeared in a field to the north of the castle, and, in September 1993 she glided across the courtyard.

Geoff described the White Lady thus: 'She was about 5 feet 4 inches tall and wearing old fashioned clothes - a white flowing dress with billowing sleeves. I have never seen her face. It appears distorted - a blur.

'There is also an odour about her - a smell of scent - but it is hard to describe. She didn't make a sound as she moved. The first time I saw her it was a little strange.'

My search for more information on the White Lady of Edzell took me to the Lindsay family vault in the nearby cemetery.

I peered through the iron railings into the tomb where the good lady rose from the dead. This time the only thing to stir was a startled wood pigeon.

Chapter Twenty-nine

The Lecht Phantom

In the gathering dusk a lone motor cyclist began a homeward journey from Deeside that would take him on the long precipitous climb back over the Lecht road.

The unpredictable Highland weather changed and a violent storm swept down on Wullie Wright as he reached 'Briggies', the last hostelry before Tomintoul. The rider sheltered at the inn, long enough to change into his waders, button up his Belstaff storm coat and adjust his goggles and peaked cap.

Despite the atrocious conditions Wullie and his new 250cc radial valve Rudge mastered the 1:3 gradient, and he reached the summit safely.

The wind buffeted the rider as he negotiated the narrow road. It was with great relief that he completed the descent from the summit, and passed the Well o' the Lecht, the halfway mark dating back to the Forty-Five Uprising.

But a mile into the second half of the journey, the bike suddenly veered on to the tricky grass centre dividing the two hard tracks. The rear wheel lost traction and both machine and rider slithered to a halt.

Wullie was horrified to find the rear tyre partially deflated.

The beam of the headlight picked out a shepherd's bothy standing just off the road.

Visibility was poor but the pale sword of light silhouetted what appeared to be a shadowy figure making its way towards the door and disappearing within.

Wullie's brother, David H. Wright, who now lives in Sussex, takes up the story: 'On reaching the building Wullie propped the bike against the wall and with some effort, prised open the heavy door which was hanging on its one remaining rusty hinge. Once inside he hoisted the bike on to its central stand and wrenched the door closed'

The place was empty, the earthen floor showed no sign of recent habitation. He got no reply to his challenge, so he set about an unenviable task.

Wullie Wright switched off the headlight to conserve the

battery, then placed a torch on the saddle to provide enough light to carry out repairs.

A violent gust shook the old door. Slates clattered off the roof.

The torch rolled off the saddle, and cut out when it hit the floor. Wullie groped around in vain for the torch. Instead he picked up the tyre pump which had been firmly secured to the chaincase.

'All hope of repairing the puncture had now faded,' said David Wright, 'and in desperation he again rotated the wheel until he located the inflation valve, connected the pump and tried to re-inflate the tyre. To his surprise the tyre quickly resumed normal pressure. He hastily stuffed the pump inside his coat and sitting astride the bike, eased it forward off the stand. This last operation usually required some effort to overcome a geometric lock before the stand would retract, but now it ran freely as if being pushed from behind.'

Wullie prodded the engine into life, but when he switched on the headlight he was confronted with a closed door. He was about to dismount when the heavy door swung open, Wullie did not waste a moment as he sped out into the clear night and completed the journey home.

The next day Wullie led David and some friends back to the mystery cottage. Before setting out, they had examined the Rudge. The offending tyre was again deflated, and the source of the problem located.

When the group arrived at the bothy they found the door shut. It was then that Tom, a colleague, who regularly used the road, told them of the cottage's haunted reputation.

The bothy was known locally as 'The Shooting Lodge', where army deserter Francis Percy Toplis, the so-called 'Monocled Mutineer', took refuge from the law after the death of an Andover taxi driver in April 1920.

A local farmer, John Grant, spotted smoke from the chimney and reported a trespasser to the laird's gamekeeper, John Mackenzie. They fetched Constable George Greig of Tomintoul and all three returned to the bothy. Toplis was lying on a bed of heather, his head propped on his jacket. He had burned furniture to heat himself. He sprang into action, cold-bloodedly shooting and wounding Grant and Greig. Mackenzie dived for cover as further shots peppered the interior walls. Toplis fled on his bike, which he sold for £1 at Strathdon. A local minister gave him a lift by car to

Aberdeen, where he boarded a train. His criminal career ended at Penrith, Cumbria, when he was ambushed in the village churchyard by armed policemen.

A decade later, the group of motor cyclists and amateur ghosthunters discussed Wullie's strange experience.

David Wright, writing in 1992, said: 'The door was subjected to a thorough scrutiny, being viewed from all angles and dragged open and closed several times, each operation increasing the strain on the rusty hinge.

'It was finally agreed that the door could not move without some extraneous force being applied. Tom at this point reminded the company that the storm had abated before Wullie had left the bothy, and yet the door had somehow swung open on its own accord!

'As each member realised the significance of this statement, there was a casual but perceptible movement towards the exit. Just as the last to leave stepped over the threshold and quickened his pace to join the others, the old door crashed to the floor amidst a cloud of dust and rotten timber. We stood transfixed for a split second and with one accord, moved off briskly, boarded our bikes and headed for home.

'The Lecht Ghost was never mentioned again. Tom always found an excuse for using the alternative route for future excursions. He would never again venture over the Lecht on a dark night alone.'

What caused the strange events on the Lecht road that stormy Saturday night in 1932? Is the bothy haunted by the ghost of Percy Toplis, or some other phantom?

Various solutions were tossed around by the bikers. Why did Wullie's bike leave the road at that exact spot? High cross winds, perhaps? The shadowy figure? The shadow of a 'passing place' marker cast by the headlight? It was agreed the tyre pump was dislodged by the heavy torch when it fell from the saddle, and a closer inspection of the floor of the cottage revealed that the bike had been slowly sinking into the soft surface. The rider's extra weight brought both wheels into contact with the ground, leaving the unloaded stand to retract freely.

And the slow leakage from the rear tyre was caused by a faulty valve. Elementary?

Wullie Wright, who served his apprenticeship as a joiner at

Cawdor Estate, and later saw action on D-Day, spent most of his working life in England. He died eight years ago.

His brother David returned to the Lecht a few summers ago. A tourist information hut occupied a spot opposite the Well o' Lecht, its inscription hidden by overgrown heather.

The bothy still stands. Its inner secrets locked and barred by a new green door.

Chapter Thirty

Journey's End

The tramcar that rattled away from the terminus in St Nicholas Street, Aberdeen, displayed the destination blind: 'SCATTERBURN'. Although it was wartime, and late evening, the tramcar was not busy. One by one the handful of passengers alighted until the conductress Nell Harper swore the tram was empty, apart from herself and the driver, George.

Suddenly the tram ground to a halt.

A frail, old woman, dressed entirely in black, boarded the 'carrie' and took a back seat on the lower deck.

Nell's curiosity was aroused but she could not distinguish the woman's face because it was concealed by a hat.

Nell recalls: 'A little while later I went to take her fare. I didn't hurry. She was sitting there. But when I got up to her she had vanished into thin air. I couldn't believe my eyes. I said to George, "Did you see that old lady when she got on the tram?" He replied, "See her? I stopped the tram abruptly to let her on!" 'Well,' I told him, 'She is not there now.'

Nell and her driver were anxious for the woman's safety for the tram had been moving at the time she vanished. 'George was in a terrible state and I said she might have broken her neck and been killed.

'We retraced the route we had come, thinking we would see her and hoping she was alright. But there was no trace of her. We couldn't get over this queer experience.'

The only explanation, added Nell, was that the old lady was the ghost of George's mother who had died sometime before.

A few weeks later Nell was waiting for George at the tram depot, prior to beginning their shift, when a colleague approached and asked: 'Who are you waiting for?' When Nell explained, back came the stunning response: 'You will have a long wait - George died suddenly this morning.'

'I couldn't believe this very sad news,' says Nell. 'I was devastated. To this day I cannot explain what we both saw that evening.'

Nell's chilling experience took place during World War Two, when, for four years, she worked on Aberdeen trams. Her workmates nicknamed her, 'The Refined Conductress'. Perhaps the soubriquet is understandable. Before the war she was house-keeper to a wealthy and influential New York family in the States.

Nell, who is in her eighties, lives in Stonehaven.

In the summer of 1958, shortly after 80,000 Aberdonians watched the last tram roll down Union Street, the entire fleet was unceremoniously burned at the Sea Beach in the dead of night.

Perhaps the flames exorcised the ghost of the Scatterburn tram?

FURTHER READING

Adams, Norman - *Haunted Valley (1994)*
Byrd, Elizabeth - *A Strange and Seeing Time (1971)*
Fraser, G. M. - *Historical Aberdeen (1905)*
Fraser, G. M. - *Aberdeen Street Names (1911)*
Grant, John - *Legends of the Braes o' Mar (1861)*
Hopkin, Archibald - *The Aberdeen Pub Companion (1975)*
Kennedy, William - *Annals of Aberdeen (1818)*
Leith-Hay, Henrietta and Marion Lochhead - *Trustie to the End (1957)*
Lewis, Roy Hartley - *Theatre Ghosts (1988)*
Low, James - *Edzell Castle Past and Present (1917)*
Mackinlay, James - *Folklore of Scottish Lochs and Springs (1893)*
Mackintosh, Herbert - *Elgin Past and Present (1914)*
Marren, Peter - *Grampian Battlefields (1990)*
McPherson, J. M. - *Primitive Beliefs in the North-east of Scotland (1929)*
Milne, John - *Myths and Superstitions of Buchan District (1881)*
Milne, John - *Aberdeen (1911)*
Orem, William - *A Description of the Chanory, Cathedral and King's College of Old Aberdeen, 1724 and 1725 (1791)*
Robertson, Joseph - *The Book of Bon-Accord (1839)*
Shaw, Lachlan - *The History of the Province of Moray (1882)*
Stirling, A.M.H. - *Fyvie Castle (1928)*
Temple, Rev William - *The Thanage of Fermartyn (1894)*
Trail, Katherine - *Reminiscences of Old Aberdeen (1932)*
The Grey Man of Ben Macdhui and Other Abnormal Happenings - Edinburgh Psychic College (1949)

OTHER SOURCES

Aberdeen Evening Express
Aberdeen Daily Journal
Cairngorm Club Journal
The Deeside Piper
Deeside Field
Dundee Courier and Advertiser
The Scotsman
Leopard Magazine

ACKNOWLEDGEMENTS

The author gratefully acknowledges the help and guidance of the following: Peter Underwood; Margaret and Christopher Christie; J.W. Irvine-Fortescue of Kingcausie; Susan Milton of Kemnay House; Captain John Hay of Delgatie; David Toulmin; David H. Wright; Lynn Montgomery; Margaret Robertson; Neil Mackenzie; K.G.Adams; Michael Ross; Fred W. White; Thomas Hendry; Ian McIntosh and Graham McIntosh, Montrose Aerdrome Museum Society; The Estate of Elizabeth Byrd; Margaret Frater; Nell Harper; John and Moyra Argo: Martin Argo; Kath Innes; Bill Harris; Edi Swan; May Cooper; Helen Leiper; Alanna and Alistair Knight; Betty Ferguson; Les Rae; Sean Stewart; Ewan Mennie; Helen and Ian McMillan of Hallgreen Castle; Geoff Hutson and David Jamieson of Historic Scotland; Roy Shirlaw; Bill McCluskey; Chevron UK Ltd., Aberdeen; Fiona and James Campbell; Anna and John Burdon; Glenda Nicol Cormack of Muchalls Castle; Geraldine Simpson; Mark Griffiths; Winifred and James Rourke; Alistair Reid; Carol and Stewart McGuire; Raymond Lamont-Brown; Sheila Angus; Gordon Mackenzie; Moray Firth Radio; Staff of The National Trust for Scotland properties at Crathes Castle, Craigievar Castle, Fyvie Castle and Leith Hall; Banff and Buchan Tourist Board; the staffs of the North-east of Scotland Library Service at Banchory and the City Arts and Recreation Division Libraries at Schoolhill and Woodside, Aberdeen; Chris and Val Norton of Pannanich Wells Hotel; The Management of the Cocket Hat, Cameron's Inn, Thunderton House, Old King's Highway, Foveran House Hotel, Ardoe House Hotel, and to those many people who willingly talked to me but wish to remain anonumous.